G. SCHIRMER'S
COLLECTION OF
OPERA LIBRETTOS

# DON CARLO

Opera in Five Acts

*Music by*

## Giuseppe Verdi

**Libretto by**
JOSEPH MERY and CAMILLE DU LOCLE

**Foreword by**
ANDREW PORTER

**English Version by**
WALTER DUCLOUX

**New English translation by**
MARY JANE MATZ

Ed. 3193

## G. SCHIRMER, Inc.

48106c

# FOREWORD

*Don Carlos* (to use the original title) was first performed at the Paris Opéra in 1867. It is the noblest and most ambitious of Verdi's operas, in which his recurrent concerns as man and as musician find their fullest statement. His championing of individual and national liberty; his detestation of political and ecclesiastical tyranny; his quick response to the tragedy of men and women in extreme plights, compelled by honor and duty to choices that destroy hopes of personal happiness; his sheer theatrical flair; and his determination to turn the paraphernalia of grand opera to a more elevated purpose than that of mere entertainment—all these come together. Five interesting characters, already linked by love, passion, and friendship in a complicated emotional pattern, are caught in a tight web of Church and State. On their deeds and decisions depend the fate of three nations—France, Spain, and Flanders—and, beyond them, of all the people in Philip II's vast empire.

Verdi was drawn to Schiller again and again by the quality Carlyle characterized as "a chivalry of thought, described by Goethe as 'the Spirit of Freedom,' struggling ever forward." A draft scenario with Schiller's *Don Carlos* as its principal source was prepared by Joseph Méry and Camille Du Locle. Verdi supervised the libretto in minute detail, working mainly with Du Locle (Méry died in 1866) and writing some of the lines himself. He added (from Schiller) the duet between Philip and Posa—that revolutionary vision of a world in which all men are free. He introduced (again from Schiller) the terrible interview between Philip and the inflexible representative of Holy Church, the Grand Inquisitor—who should be "blind and very old," Verdi said, for reasons he preferred not to commit to paper. The practical man in him insisted further on a spectacular scene with novel décor that would catch the public's fancy—something like the skating or the coronation scene from *Le Prophète*. And so the coronation-cum-*auto da fe* of Act III was added. It is, of course, more than mere spectacle, and marks the public crisis heralding the private crises of Act IV. Verdi once called it "the heart of the opera," and when he came to revise the work it was the only scene he left unchanged.

This was huge material to handle. Verdi struggled again and again to give *Don Carlos* a shape at once practicable, performable without cuts, attractive to the general public, and yet still faithful to his vision of elevated, ennobling music drama. As first conceived, the opera proved impracticably long. During the Paris rehearsals, Verdi removed some of the scenes he had composed (e.g. a duet for Elizabeth and Eboli, before "O don fatal," and another for Philip and Carlos, after the death of Posa). When the dress rehearsal still ran too long, he was forced to make a few further cuts, or else the show would continue after midnight, which was against Opéra rules. The biggest of the last-minute cuts was of the *Prélude et Introduction,* a ten-minute passage that is being restored in the current Met production. It sets the scale of the piece; it sounds both the recurrent musical motif (in the very opening measures) and the dominant themes of the drama—the relationship of ruled and rulers; the conflict between duty and personal desire.

The passages omitted in 1867 were literally cut from the autograph; they remained unpublished and until nine years ago unknown. What was left was already more than most theatres were willing to tackle. Since there were bound to be cuts, let them be those effected, however reluctantly by the composer himself. As he wrote later, while engaged on a further round of abridgment, when there had to be an operation he preferred to wield the knife himself.

Verdi declared that he had composed *Don Carlos* with the intention of "transforming our theatres." It represented a new kind of opera, he said, not a succession of numbers but the expression of a central idea; every detail—even in the ballet—

iii

had its significance, and every detail of a performance, musical or scenic, should be directed by a single intelligence. In 1872 he went to Naples to direct *Don Carlos* himself in "an accurate execution embodying all the reforms demanded by modern art." For this production he recomposed the crucial Philip-Posa duet to bring it into even sharper focus and to reinstate important exchanges that in 1867 had been omitted. (Ghislanzoni provided the new lines required.) He also took out the *marziale* section of the final duet. Others theatres continued to maltreat the work, and in 1882—when *Otello* was already beginning to take shape—he set about a thoroughgoing revision and abridgment, to make the opera, in his own words, "more practicable and also, I believe, better from an artistic point of view." He removed Act I (saving only Carlos's *romance,* which was recomposed and inserted into the following scene), the ballet, and the scene that precedes it. He restored important motivation that had disappeared in 1867. Once again he recomposed the Philip-Posa duet, in a still more powerful form. He brought the last two acts to rapid conclusions. ("All those massive choruses weigh on my stomach.") He restored the *marziale.* He tightened dialogues and ensembles but left the big solos unchanged, as expansive monologues set now in a swift-moving drama whose musical manner often adumbrates *Otello.* This revision was carried out in French, in collaboration with Du Locle, and again Verdi wrote some of the most important lines himself. The revised *Carlos* had its first performance in Italian translation, at La Scala in 1884.

Two years later there was a Modena production in which, with Verdi's consent and approval, the original, Paris Act I was added to the four revised acts, and this composite score was published, in Italian translation only. There matters rested— *Carlos* was performed in either the four-act 1884 or the five-act 1886 version, with occasional admixtures (especially in Germany and Russia) of 1867, and seldom complete—until in 1969 the Verdi scholar David Rosen turned up 42 extra measures of the Philip-Posa duet which in 1867 had been folded down in, but not physically cut from, the conducting score. A few months later I discovered the rest of the "missing" music, building it up line by line from the 1867 performance material, in which it was stitched up or pasted over, not actually removed. (A few instrumental lines needed filling in here and there.) As a result, in 1973 the BBC and the Boston Opera could both give a "more-than-complete" 1867 *Don Carlos,* including the *Prélude et Introduction,* the Elizabeth-Eboli duet, the Philip-Posa duet, and other music never done before. Since then, several productions have included some of my "new" passages, and Ricordi has now printed a variorum score, edited by Ursula Günther and Luciano Petazzoni, which includes nearly all the music ever composed for the opera in any of its versions.

There can be no "definitive" edition of *Don Carlos*—it is a matter of choosing among rich alternatives—but there can be good editions and bad editions. Bad ones, I suggest are those in which "new" music (i.e. music cut by Verdi himself) is reinstated at the expense of music that Verdi himself deemed indispensable (hearing these, I have sometimes even regretted that I did not leave those dusty 1867 parts undisturbed), those in which 1867 and 1884 are indiscriminately jumbled, and those in which an otherwise consistent text is disfigured by cuts. Verdi changed his mind several times about various points, and he was never altogether happy with the ending, but about one thing he was consistent: *Carlos,* in whatever version, should never be cut beyond the extent to which he himself had cut it. In 1883, he insisted anew that his revised score should be done in its entirety. "Be firm about this," he told Ricordi, "for I know all baritones will want to end the act with the aria; the [insurrection as recomposed] lasts only two minutes, and it's necessary." On the other hand, theatres that wanted to do the ballet were welcome to add it, he said; and in 1886 he evidently sanctioned the restoration of Act I.

At the Met, *Don Carlos* is being done uncut: i.e. none of the music Verdi chose to retain is being removed, and none of his revisions are replaced by unrevised passages. Act I (which he never revised) will be heard as he conceived it; it is not disfigured by the all-too-common cut in the Elizabeth-Carlos duet, and it further includes the important *Prélude et Introduction.* Acts II to V are done as he established them in

iv

1882-83, without the cuts of a stanza here, an episode there, all too often made, and without interpolations that belong to a different version of the score. (One qualification: since Carlos can hardly sing his *romance* twice over, it retains its original form and position, in Act I.) This is a consistent, expansive version of *Don Carlos,* and I believe it is the best possible one for a large company with large resources.

*Don Carlos* had its American premiere at the New York Academy of Music in 1877. It was first performed at the Metropolitan Opera, in 1920, with Ponselle, Matzenauer, Martinelli, De Luca, and Didur. There was a new production in 1950, with Delia Rigal, Barbieri, Björling, Merrill, and Siepi, conductor Stiedry, director Margaret Webster, designer Rolf Gérard, and this was last seen in 1972. All these productions were given in Italian translation.

Andrew Porter

# DON CARLO

A self-proclaimed apostle of the Italian dramatist Vittorio Alfieri, Verdi absorbed many of the political values of this spokesman for the republican movement in Italy. Thus it is natural that *Don Carlo* draws heavily on Alfieri's *Filippo* for its feeling and color. In the period 1823-1832, when Verdi was still a schoolboy, he discovered Alfieri, whose dramas were considered "dangerous" because of their revolutionary views. Alfieri preached (among other doctrines) regicide, which Verdi would later use as a motivation in such works as *Rigoletto, Macbeth,* and *Un Ballo in maschera.* Impelled toward an Alfierian political stance even before he was 20, Verdi made his own Milanese debut not in an opera house, but in the Teatro dei Filodrammatici, known earlier as the Teatro Patriottico, where Alfieri's *Brutus, Filippo* and *Virginia* were produced, before the authorities shut down the theatre for political reasons.

Verdi's own children were named Icilio and Virginia, for protagonists created by Alfieri; and Verdi's *Don Carlo* bears certain clearly identifiable debts to *Filippo.* These are Verdi's "real debts," those which have to do with his origins, and his first studies, for the Alfieri drama is accented with certain "theatrical words" (to use Verdi's own term) such as "blind love," "terror," "doubt," "shadow," "this horrible palace," "darkness," and "the oppression of innocent people" which give *Don Carlo* its particular fearsome quality.

Even Verdi's wife brought her own "debts" to *Don Carlo,* for the godfather of her first child was Luigi Vestri, Italy's greatest nineteenth-century actor, who played a leading role in the world premiere of Alfieri's *Filippo,* in the playwright's own house.

The immediate and more frequently studied source of *Don Carlo* is Schiller's *Don Carlos,* the fourth of the German playwright's works which Verdi had used as a base for creating the librettos of his operas. At the time that Verdi was thinking about writing a "new work," he was searching frantically for the right libretto. He begged his friends in France to help. "A libretto, a libretto and the work is done!" he wrote in June, 1865.

He had never been under heavier fire. His own publisher and some of Europe's most serious critics had praised Faccio's opera *Hamlet* (now forgotten) without reservation. "In forty years, Italy has not seen such a complete opera, such a modern and refined work," wrote the major Italian critic. Even one of Verdi's closest friends, the great conductor Angelo Mariani, had turned against him (or so it seemed to the composer), by directing Faccio's *Hamlet.*

"They are all clowns," Verdi said, with typical terseness.

But the fever was in him—to compose another major work.

He had sworn that he would "never, absolutely never" write another opera for the Paris Opéra, where huge stage machinery, a lumbering bureaucracy and endless rehearsals sapped his energy. But in the summer of 1865, when his French publisher brought him a firm proposal for a new opera, Verdi agreed to write *Don Carlos* (as it was called for the original French Paris version). Verdi signed the contract in December; four months earlier he had given up his seat in the Italian Parliament.

Here was a full-scale commitment to the opera which would prove to everyone that "Verdi was still Verdi." All five acts of the opera were finished in draft by July, 1866; and, as was Verdi's wont, the orchestration was completed and changes were made after the vocal rehearsals began. The premiere took place on March 11, 1867. Verdi left Paris at once, with his wife, to take possession of their new apartment in Palazzo Sauli-Pallavicino in Genoa. This is the house the Verdis shared with the conductor Angelo Mariani, one of the most famous musicians of the century, a man who worshipped Verdi.

The Paris premiere aroused a mixed response in the audience and critics — a cool reception, on the whole. But Mariani, who had immediately offered to redeem Verdi's other "failure," *La Traviata*, hurried to Verdi's side to "save" *Don Carlos*, since other composers, like Bizet, were accusing Verdi of "no longer being Italian." Verdi, in turn, denounced the "anemic and frigid" Paris public, and agreed to let Mariani produce *Don Carlo* (to give the opera its new Italian name) in Bologna. In August, 1867, Verdi, his wife and Mariani set out again for Paris, where Mariani saw the Opéra production and planned his own.

The premiere of what is known as *Don Carlo* (the Italian translation of the original French work) took place in June, 1867 in London. But the Bologna premiere, under Mariani's direction, October 27, 1867, the first indisputable, overwhelming triumph for *Don Carlo*, was the performance which launched the opera on what has become its enduring life as a part of the permanent repertory.

Verdi, who had written "Now that my career is over . . ." (earlier in 1867), became the composer of the hour once again. From this collaboration with Mariani and the Teatro Comunale in Bologna, it was but a short step to the *Requiem* and *Aida*, then to *Otello* and *Falstaff*. The impulse to give up, to retire, had been overcome and the drive to compose aroused once more.

Mary Jane Matz

# THE STORY

ACT I, Scene 1. In the forest of the King, near the palace of Fontainebleau, wood-cutters and their wives have gathered around a bonfire. They lament their lives, their poverty and the strife which war with Spain has brought upon France. When a hunting party from the palace approaches, they beg the princess, Elizabeth of Valois, to help a desperate widow who has lost both her sons in the fighting. Elizabeth gives her a gold chain, and begs them all to take courage. The treaty of peace is almost concluded, she says, and their wretched condition will change. She leaves with the hunters.

Suddenly the Spanish prince Don Carlo steps from the shelter of the dark forest. At last he has caught a glimpse of Elizabeth his betrothed. He sings of his love for the woman who will be his bride. Lost, and separated from the hunting party, Elizabeth and her page Tebaldo appear. Don Carlo salutes her, and offers to protect her. She sends her page away. Revealing his love, he gives her a miniature of himself. For the first time, Elizabeth realizes that Don Carlo is the man she is pledged to marry. They rejoice over their shared love, which brings peace to their nations. Suddenly, the sound of a cannon is heard. Elizabeth's page returns, hailing her as the betrothed of King Philip II, not the bride of Don Carlo. In horror, she recoils from Tebaldo, crying that she is pledged to the King's son. But the page insists that as part of a treaty she has been promised to King Philip, and will reign as Queen of Spain. As woodcutters and hunters joyfully greet the news that peace has come, Elizabeth and Don Carlo, crushed by despair, sing that their love is doomed.

ACT II, Scene 1. Don Carlo seeks consolation at the cloister of the Monastery of St. Just, where the monks chant their prayers at the tomb of Charles V, Don Carlo's grandfather. His friend Rodrigo, Marquis of Posa, suggests that Carlo leave for the Netherlands, to cure himself of his infatuation and to protect the Flemish against the tyranny of Spain. The two men pledge friendship; King Philip and Queen Elizabeth approach the tomb, kneel briefly and proceed on their way.

Scene 2. In the cloister garden, Princess Eboli, the Countess of Aremberg and their ladies entertain themselves; Eboli sings a Moorish song to the accompaniment of Tebaldo's mandolin. As the Queen enters from the monastery, Rodrigo appears, hands her a letter from Don Carlo and tells her that the Prince longs to see her. Elizabeth agrees to receive him, and the page leads Don Carlo to her side. The ladies retire. Don Carlo begs the Queen to obtain Philip's leave for him to go to Flanders and then declares his love in a passionate avowal. Breaking free of Don Carlo's embrace, Elizabeth turns him away. No sooner has he left than Philip reenters with his suite, and finding his wife unattended, banishes the Countess of Aremberg, who should have been at the Queen's side. Elizabeth consoles her; the ladies depart, leaving Rodrigo to plead the Flemish cause with Philip. The King suspects that Elizabeth and Don Carlo may have betrayed him and asks Rodrigo to watch the lovers, warning him of the Grand Inquisitor's enmity.

ACT III, Scene 1. At midnight Don Carlo awaits the Queen in her garden in Madrid, following the instructions in a letter written, he believes, by Elizabeth but in reality penned by Eboli, who mistakenly thinks Don Carlo loves her. When the veiled Eboli enters, Don Carlo passionately declares his love; when she unveils, both realize their error. Furiously she accuses him of loving the Queen. Rodrigo comes upon them, grasps the situation and tries to placate Eboli, who runs from the garden swearing to expose Don Carlo and Elizabeth. To protect the Prince, Rodrigo takes certain incriminating papers from him.

ix

Scene 2. In the square before the Cathedral of Our Lady of Atocha, in Madrid, an immense crowd awaits the auto-da-fé and appearance of King Philip. The monarch emerges from the church and is greeted by six Flemish deputies led by Don Carlo. Prince, populace and court plead for the King's mercy, but the friars insist on punishment for his rebellious subjects. Drawing his sword, Don Carlo swears to champion the Flemish cause in defiance of his father, who orders him disarmed. But Don Carlo surrenders his sword to Rodrigo, while all watch a group of heretics being burned at the stake. A celestial voice welcomes their souls into heaven.

ACT IV, Scene 1. In his study Philip laments his wife's coldness. He then consults with the Inquisitor, who urges the death of both Don Carlo and Rodrigo. As the old man leaves, the King muses regretfully that the throne must always yield to the church. Elizabeth bursts in, crying that her jewel casket has been stolen. Philip hands it to her with an ironic demand that she open it. When she hesitates, he breaks the lock, revealing a portrait of Don Carlo. He accuses her of adultery. The Queen faints as Eboli and Rodrigo enter, the former confessing responsibility for Elizabeth's betrayal, the latter swearing to free Spain from political oppression. When the men have left, Eboli reveals to the Queen that she gave the casket to Philip out of jealousy over Don Carlo's love and that she has been the King's mistress. Banishing Eboli to life in a convent or exile, Elizabeth leaves her. The remorseful Princess laments her fatal beauty and swears to save Don Carlo's life.

Scene 2. Rodrigo visits Don Carlo in prison and is shot to death by an official of the Inquisition. As he dies, he tells Carlo that Elizabeth will await him at the cloister to bid farewell. Philip enters and gives Carlo back his sword but Carlo repulses him as the murderer of his faithful friend, whose death Philip now laments. A crowd of citizens storms the prison demanding Carlo's release, and the disguised Eboli urges Carlo to flee. The Grand Inquisitor appears and demands that the rebellious crowd kneel in obedience before Philip.

ACT V. In the monastery cloister Elizabeth waits to bid farewell to Don Carlo. The lovers are surprised by Philip and the Grand Inquisitor, but Don Carlo is protected from them both when the ghostly Charles V emerges from the tomb and draws him into the shadows of the cloister.

*Courtesy of Opera News*

*Note:* The Metropolitan Opera's performing version of *Don Carlo* differs in some respects from the stage instructions contained in this libretto. In addition, the first and second acts are presented as Act I; the third act is presented as Act II and the fourth and fifth acts are presented as Act III.

# CAST OF CHARACTERS

PHILIP II, King of Spain . . . . . . . . . . . . . . . . Bass

DON CARLO, Crown Prince of Spain . . . . . . . . . . Tenor

RODRIGO, Marquis of Posa . . . . . . . . . . . . . Baritone

THE GRAND INQUISITOR . . . . . . . . . . . . . . . Bass

THE COUNT OF LERMA . . . . . . . . . . . . . . . Tenor

A FRIAR . . . . . . . . . . . . . . . . . . . . . . Bass

ELIZABETH OF VALOIS, Daughter of Henry II, King of France . . . Soprano

THE PRINCESS OF EBOLI . . . . . . . . . . Mezzo-Soprano

TEBALDO, Elizabeth's Page . . . . . . . . . . . . . Soprano

THE COUNTESS OF AREMBERG . . . . . . . . . . . . Mute

A ROYAL HERALD . . . . . . . . . . . . . . . . . Tenor

A CELESTIAL VOICE . . . . . . . . . . . . . . . Soprano

A FORESTER . . . . . . . . . . . . . . . . . . . Bass

French Woodsmen and Huntsmen, Flemish Deputies, Inquisitors, Gentlemen and Ladies of the Court of Spain, Pages, Guards of Philip II, Friars, Members of the Holy Office, Soldiers, Magistrates, Deputies from the Colonies of the Spanish Empire, etc.

TIME: France and Spain, c. 1560

# SYNOPSIS OF SCENES

# DON CARLO

## ATTO PRIMO

(*La foresta di Fontainebleau. Inverno. A destra, un grande masso forma una specie de antro. In fondo in lontananza, il palazzo reale.*)

(*I boscaioli, le loro moglie e i loro bambini. Alcuni sono occupati; le donne e i fanciulli si scaldano a un fuoco acceso. Lamentano la loro povertà e disperazione.*)

#### I BOSCAIOLI E LE LORO MOGLIE

L'inverno è lungo; il pane è caro.
La vita è dura.
Mai più finirà il tuo gelo,
O inverno amaro?
Ahimè! Terminerà la guerra?
Ahimè! Li rivedremo mai?
Rivedremo ritornare i figli nostri
Ai casolari e i campi arati maturar?
Quì di freddo e fame si muore;
E giù al piano il fiume ghiacciò,
Dell'inverno il grando rigore
L'acque gelò di Fontainebleau!
Ahimè!

#### UN UOMO

Amici, ritorniamo al lavoro!
Per le spose, i figli facciamoci coraggio!
La pace a noi lavoratori donerà dei dì
  migliori.
(*Delle fanfare risuonano nella foresta.*)
(*Voci da lontano*)

#### I CACCIATORI

A sinistra! A destra!
A sinistra! A destra!

#### I BOSCAIOLI

Sentite là! La tromba chiama!
Sentite là? Risponde il corno!
La Corte a caccia verrà.
Della caccia il Re sarà!
(*delle fanfare*)

#### I CACCIATORI
(*Da lontano*)

Su, cacciator! Pronti o la belva ci
  sfuggirà,
E noi l'avrem pria ch'alla selva notte
  verrà.

#### I CACCIATORI E LE LORO MOGLI

Il suon dei corni s'avvicina,
Echeggian grida d'ogni parte;
Chi più di loro felice è?
Fortunata è la sorte dei Re!

(*Boscaioli, cacciatori. Elisabetta di Valois appare, a cavallo, condotta da Tebaldo, suo paggio. Valletti e battistrada.*)

#### I BOSCAIOLI E LE LORO MOGLI

È la figlia del Re!
Presto! Ci appressiamo a lei.
Non è meno buona che bella,
La nobile Elisabetta!

#### ELISABETTA
(*Arrestando il suo cavallo*)
Amici, che mi chiedete?

#### TUTTI
(*conducendo una donna in lutto alla presenza di Elisabetta*)
Noi non vi supplichiam per noi, ma
  soccorrete la miseria
Di questa vedova i cui due figli chiamati
  in guerra per il Re!
Ah! Pietà di lei! Pietà di lei!
Non tornarono più!

#### ELISABETTA
(*alla povera donna*)
Accetta, buona madre, questa catena
  d'or.

(*ai boscaioli*)
E voi tutti sperate;
Ben presto questa guerra finirà.
Dei bei dì per noi verranno ancora.
Presso Re Enrico, mio padre, un messo
  il Re di Spagna inviò;
Con la pace ormai, se Dio vorrà, tornerà
  la serenità.

1

# DON CARLO

## ACT ONE

*(The forest of Fontainebleau. Winter. At the right, a large rock-mass forms a kind of shelter. In the distance, the royal palace.)*

*(Woodcutters are working; their wives are gathered around a bonfire, lamenting their poverty and despair.)*

#### WOODCUTTERS AND THEIR WIVES

The winter is long; bread is expensive.
Will your chill season ever end,
O dark winter?
Alas! Will the war end?
Alas! Shall we ever see our sons
Come back from war, and our wheat
Ripen in our fields?
Here, we are dying of cold and hunger;
In the plain, the river is frozen;
And cruel winter freezes over the waters
 of Fontainebleau! Alas!

#### MAN

Friends, let us get to work at once!
For our women and children, let us take
 heart.
When peace comes, we laborers shall see
 better days.

*(The sound of trumpets is heard from far away.)*

*(Voices offstage)*

#### HUNTERS' CRIES

To the left! To the right!
To the left! To the right!

#### WOODCUTTERS

Do you hear that? The sound of a
 trumpet!
Do you hear that? The hunting horn
 calling!
The court has left the palace!
The King has come out to hunt!
*(another fanfare of trumpets)*

#### HUNTERS *(offstage)*

On, hunter! Quickly!
The stag is getting away in the under-
 brush. We will lose him.
We shall get the stag while we have day-
 light in the woods!

#### WOODSMAN AND THEIR WIVES

The sound of horns is nearer,
Echoing on every side.
Who is happier than they?
Kings always have good fortune!

*(Woodsmen and hunters onstage. Elizabeth of Valois appears, on horseback, led by her page, Tebaldo. She is accompanied by her entourage and by beaters.)*

#### WOODCUTTERS AND THEIR WIVES

There is the King's daughter!
Quick! Let us approach her;
She is as good as she is beautiful,
This noble Elizabeth!

#### ELIZABETH
*(reining in her horse)*

My friends, what do you want?

#### ALL
*(leading a woman dressed in mourning to Elizabeth)*

We beg you for help, not for ourselves,
 but for this wretched widow,
Whose two sons were called up by the
 King for the army.
Have pity on her! Have pity on her!
Her sons will never return home!

#### ELIZABETH
*(to the Poor Woman)*

Good woman, I give you this gold chain.
*(to the Woodsmen)*
As for all of you, keep up your hopes;
This war will soon end.
We will again enjoy good times.
A Spanish envoy of the King has come
 to seek my father, King Henry;
If God is willing, peace and serenity shall
 reign once more.

1

CORO

O Signora, che Dio vi doni,
Leggendo in fondo al nostro cuor,
Un giovin sposo e la corona,
E d'un popolo l'amor.
La pace, a noi lavoratori, donerà dei
   dì migliori!

CORO INTERNO DI CACCIATORI

Su, cacciator! Pronti o la belva ci
   sfuggirà!
E noi l'avrem, pria ch'alla selva notte
verrà. L'inseguiam.

(ELISABETTA *traversa la scena in mezzo al suono delle fanfare, e getta delle
monete ai boscaiuoli.* DON CARLO
*appare a sinistar nascondendosi fra
gli alberi. I* BOSCAIUOLI *guardano la*
PRINCIPESSA *che si allontana, e ripren-
dendo i loro utensili si mettono in
cammino, e si disperdono pei sentieri
del fondo.*)

DON CARLO

Fontainebleau! foresta immensa e so-
   litaria!
Quai giardin, quai rosai, qual Eden di
   splendore
Per Don Carlo potrà questo bosco valer,
Ove Elisabetta sua sorridente apparì!
Lasciai l'Iberia, la corte lasciai,
Di Filippo sfidando il tremendo furore.
Confuso nel corteo del regio Amba-
   sciador;
Potei mirarl'alfin, la bella fidanzata!
Colei che vidi pria regnar sull'alma mia.
Colei che per l'amor regnerà sul mio cor!
Io la vidi e al suo sorriso
Scintillar mi parve il sole;
Come l'alma al paradiso
Schiuse a lei la speme il vol.
Tanta gioia a me prometto
Che s'innebria questo cor;
Dio, sorridi al nostro affetto,
Benedici una casto amor.

(DON CARLO *corre sulle tracce d'*ELIS-
ABETTA; *ma s'arresta incerto ed
ascolta. Un suono di corno si fa udir
di lontano, poi tutto ritorna nel silenzio.*)

Il suon del corno alfin nel bosco tace.
   (*ascoltando*)
Non più dei cacciator echeggiano i
   clamor!
Cadde il dì! Tace ognun! E la stella
   primiera
Scintilla nel lontan spazio azzurrin.
Come del regio ostel rinvenire il cam-
   min?
Questa selva è tanto nera!

TEBALDO (*di dentro*)
Olà scudier! olà! paggi del Re!

DON CARLO
Qual voce risuonò nell'oscura foresta?

TEBALDO
Olà venite, boscaiuoli, a me!
(TEBALDO *ed* ELIZABETTA *scendono da
un sentiero.*)

DON CARLO
(*Ritirandosi in disparte*)
Oh! vision gentile, ver me s'avanza!

TEBALDO (*con terrore*)
Non trovo più la via per ritornar...
Ecco il mio braccio; sostegno a voi fia.
La notte è buia, il gel vi fa tremar;
Andiam ancor...

ELISABETTA
Ahi! come stanca sono!
(DON CARLO *appare e s'inchina ad*
ELISABETTA.)

TEBALDO
(*Atterrito a* DON CARLO)
Ciel! ma chi sei tu?

DON CARLO (*ad* ELISABETTA)
Io sono uno stranier, uno spagnuol.

## CHORUS

Noble Lady, may God read the prayers
   in our hearts,
And bring you a young husband, a
   crown,
And the love of a happy people.
When peace comes, oh, workers, we shall
   see better days!

## HUNTERS

*(again from backstage)*

On, hunter! Quickly!
The stag is getting away in the under-
   brush. We will lose him!
We will get him before night falls in the
   forest.

*(The Princess Elizabeth rides away,
throwing money to the Woodcutters.
They take up their tools and disappear
into the woods. Fanfares are heard,
farther and farther away. Don Carlo
steps from the cover of the woods into
the clearing.)*

## DON CARLO

Fontainebleau!
Immense and lonely forest!
No garden, no rose-bower,
No resplendent Eden
Can mean more to Don Carlo
Than this lonely woods,
Where his radiant Princess stood!
I left Spain; I fled the Court
Of King Philip, defying his terrible rage,
Fleeing hidden among the courtiers
   the royal ambassador;
At last I have been able to see her,
My beautiful betrothed!
She whom I saw just now
Rules over my spirit;
She, with her love,
Shall rule over my heart!
I saw her, and when she smiled,
I thought I saw the sparkling sun;
As the soul flies to Paradise,
My hopes and joy fly towards her.
I promise myself so much joy
That my heart bursts with rapture;
God, smile upon our affection,
Bless this chaste love.

*(Don Carlo follows Elizabeth's path; but
he stops, hesitating, and listens. From
afar, the sound of a horn is heard, then
silence.)*

## DON CARLO

The sound of the hunting horn can no
   longer be heard. *(listening)*
There is no more noise of the hunters.
Day is dying! All is still!
And the first star of evening
Shines in the far-off blue sky.
How will I find again the path that leads
   to the palace?
The forest is so dark!

## TEBALDO *(offstage)*

Ho, there! Squires! Royal pages!

## DON CARLO

Whose voice can that be, in the depths of
   the forest?

## TEBALDO

Ho, there! Woodcutters, come here!

*(Tebaldo and Elizabeth come down a
path.)*

## DON CARLO *(drawing back, out of sight)*

Oh! What a beautiful vision comes
   towards me!

## TEBALDO *(terrified)*

I can no longer find the way back.
Here, take my arm. Let me help you.
The night is dark; and you are trembling
   from the cold.
Let us go on.

## ELIZABETH *(cries out)*

Ah! How tired I am!

*(Don Carlo appears and kneels before
Elizabeth.)*

## TEBALDO

*(terrified, seeing Don Carlo)*

Heavens! Who are you?

## DON CARLO *(addressing Elizabeth)*

I am a stranger, a Spaniard.

ELISABETTA (*vivamente*)

Di quei del corteo ch'accompagnan
Il signore di Lerma, Ambasciator di
Spagna?

DON CARLO (*con foco*)

Sì, nobil donna. E scudo a voi sarò.

TEBALDO

(*In fondo al teatro*)

Qual piacer! brillar lontano
Laggiù mirai Fontainebleau.
Per ricondurvi al regio ostello
Sino al castel io correrò.

ELISABETTA (*con autorità*)

Va, non temer per me:
La regal fidanzata di Don Carlo son io!
Ho fe' nell'onore spagnuol!
Paggio, al castel t'affretta!

(*mostrando* DON CARLO)

Ei difender saprà la figlia del tuo Re.
(DON CARLO *la saluta, e, la mano sulla
spada, si pone dignitosamente alla
destra d'*ELISABETTA. TEBALDO *s'inchina ed esce dal fondo.*)
(ELISABETTA *si pone a sedere sopra un
masso di roccia ed alza lo sguardo su
*DON CARLO *in piedi innanzi ad essa.
*DON CARLO *rompe alcuni ramoscelli
sparsi a terra ed avviva il fuoco.*)

ELISABETTA

(*sorpresa*)

Al mio piè perchè!

DON CARLO

Alla guerra, quando il ciel per tenda
abbiam,
Sterpi chiedere alla terra per la fiamma
noi dobbiam!
Già, già la stipa diè la bramata scintilla,
E la fiamma ecco già brilla.
Al campo allor che splende così vivace
e bella
La messaggiera ell'è di vittoria, d'amor.

ELISABETTA

E lasciaste Madrid?

DON CARLO

Sì.

ELISABETTA

Conchiuder questa sera la pace si potrà?

DON CARLO

Sì, pria del dì novel stipular l'imeneo
Col figlio del mio Re, con Don Carlo
si dè.

ELISABETTA

Ah! favelliam di lui.
Ah! Terror arcano invade questo core
Esul lontana andrò, la Francia lascierò!
Ma pari al mio vorrei di lui l'amore.

DON CARLO

Carlo vorrà viver al vostro piè,
Arde d'amore; nel vostro cor ha fè.

ELISABETTA

Io lascierò la Francia e il padre insieme;
Dio lo vuol, partirò; un'altra patria avrò,
N'andrò giuliva e pieno il cor di speme.

DON CARLO

E Carlo pur amandovi vivrà
Al vostro piè lo giuro, ei v'amerà.

ELISABETTA

Perchè mi balza il cor? Ciel! chi siete
mai?

DON CARLO

(*Dandole una busta ornata di gemme.*)

Del prence messagger, per voi questo
recai.

ELISABETTA

Un suo don!

DON CARLO

V'inviò l'immagin sua fedel, noto vi
fia così.

ELIZABETH (*eagerly*)

One of the courtiers who have come
With Count Lerma, the Spanish
　Ambassador?

DON CARLO (*with much emotion*)

Yes, noble lady! And I will protect you.

TEBALDO (*from the rear*)

What joy! I see the lights of Fontaine-
　bleau, down there, but far away.
I will run ahead, to lead you to the royal
　palace.

ELIZABETH (*with regal authority*)

Go! Do not be afraid for me.
I am the royal princess, betrothed
To Don Carlo! I trust the honor of a
　Spaniard!
Hurry to the palace, then, Page!
He will defend the daughter of your
　King. (*indicating Carlo*)

(*Don Carlo salutes her; his hand on his
sword, he steps to Elizabeth's right,
with great dignity. Tebaldo kneels and
leaves. Elizabeth sits down on a rocky
spur, and raises her eyes to Don Carlo,
who stands before her. Don Carlo
breaks up some branches and starts a
fire. Suddenly, he looks at Elizabeth
and kneels.*)

ELIZABETH (*surprised*)

Why do you kneel before me?

DON CARLO

In time of war, when the sky is our tent,
　we have to beg the earth to give us
　brushwood for our fire.
See there! The brush has given the fire a
　needed spark,
And the flames rise.
In our camp, when the fire burns like
　this,
Beautiful and bright,
It promises us victory, or love.

ELIZABETH

And you have left Madrid?

DON CARLO

Yes.

ELIZABETH

Will the treaty of peace
Be concluded tonight?

DON CARLO

Yes, before dawn tomorrow, the
　marriage must be arranged
With Don Carlo, the son of my King.

ELIZABETH

Ah, let us talk together.
Let us talk about him.
A strange terror has invaded my heart,
I will leave France, go to a faraway
　exile;
But I pray that his love is as great as
　mine.

DON CARLO

Carlo will want to live beside you;
He is afire with love;
Let your heart trust him.

ELIZABETH

I will leave France, and my father;
God wills it so; I shall go;
Another country will be my country.
I go there joyfully, my heart filled with
　hope.

DON CARLO

And Carlo, too, will live for love of you,
　will live beside you, and will love you.

ELIZABETH

Why does my heart beat like this?
Heaven! Who are you?

DON CARLO

(*He gives her a jewelled case.*)
　The Prince's messenger; I brought you
　this.

ELIZABETH

A gift from him!

DON CARLO

He sent you this true likeness of himself,
You may know him from this.

ELISABETTA

Gran Dio! io lo vedrò!
Non oso aprir . . .
Ah! ma pur vederlo bramo . . .
(*Guarda il ritratto e riconosce* DON
CARLO.)
Possente Iddio!

DON CARLO

(*Cadendo à suoi piedi*)

Carlo son io . . . e t'amo, sì t'amo!

ELISABETTA

(*tra sè*)

(Di qual amor, di quant'ardor
Questa'alma è piena!
Al suo destin voler divin
Or m'incatena . . .
Arcan terror m'avea nel cor,
E ancor ne tremo.
Amata io son, gaudio supremo
Ne sento in cor!)

DON CARLO

Sì, t'amo, te sola io bramo,
Vivrò per te, per te morrò.

ELISABETTA

Se l'amor ci guidò, se a me t'avvicinò
Il fè perchè ci vuol felici appieno.
(*S' ode il tuonar lontano del cannone.*)
Qual rumor!

DON CARLO

Il cannone echeggiò.

ELISABETTA

Fausto dì!
Questo è segnal di festa!

DON CARLO E ELISABETTA

Sì, lode al ciel, la pace è stretta!
(*I veroni illuminati di Fontainebleau
brillano in lontananza.*)

ELISABETTA

Qual baglior!
È il castel che risplende così.

DON CARLO

(*Stringendo* ELISABETTA *fra le braccia*)

Sparì l'orror della foresta;
Tutto è gioia, splendor,
Tutto è delizia, amor.

ELISABETTA E DON CARLO

Il ciel ci vegga alfin uniti cor a cor
Nell'imeneo che Dio ci appresta.

DON CARLO

Ah! non temer, ritorna in te.
O bella fidanzata! Angel d'amor,
Leva su me la tua pupilla amata.

ELISABETTA

Se tremo ancor, terror non è,
Mi sento già rinata!
A voluttà nuova per me
È l'alma abbandonata.

ELISABETTA E DON CARLO

Rinnovelliam ebbri d'amor
Il giuro che ci univa;
Lo disse il labbro, il ciel l'udiva,
Lo fece il cor.
(TEBALDO *entra coi* PAGGI, *portando
fiaccole. I* PAGGI *restano nel fondo.*
TEBALDO *s'avanza solo verso* ELISA-
BETTA.)

TEBALDO

(*Prostrandosi e baciando la veste
d'* ELISABETTA)

Al fedel ch'ora viene, o signora,
Un messaggio felice a recar,
Accordate un favor; di serbarmi con voi
Nè mai lasciarvi più.

ELISABETTA

(*Facendogli cenno d'alzarsi*)

Sia pur!

TEBALDO

Regina, vi saluto, sposa a Filippo re.

ELIZABETH

Good God! I shall see him!
I dare not open it! Ah!
But I want to see him!
(*She opens the case and recognizes him.*)
Great God!

DON CARLO (*falling at her feet*)

I am Carlo and I love you!
I love you!

ELIZABETH (*to herself*)

This soul of mine is filled
With such love, with such burning
    passion!
I bind myself now to his fate, to his
    divine will!
Strange terror filled my heart,
    it makes me tremble still.
I am loved! I am loved! I feel
    sublime joy in my heart!

DON CARLO

Yes, I love you; I love you. I want only
    you.
I shall live and die for you.

ELIZABETH

If love has brought us here,
If love has sent you to me,
It wants us to be utterly happy.
(*The sound of a cannon is heard in the
    distance*)
What noise!

DON CARLO

The sound of a cannon.

ELIZABETH

Joyful day!
This is the signal for rejoicing!

ELIZABETH AND DON CARLO

Yes, heaven be praised!
Peace is settled.
(*The large, lighted windows of Fon-
    tainebleau shine in the distance.*)

ELIZABETH

See the lights!
That is the palace.

DON CARLO

(*holding Elizabeth in his arms*)
Let the terror of the forest be put aside
    forever.
All is joy and splendor, delight and love.

ELIZABETH AND DON CARLO

Heaven be our witness, as we are united,
    our hearts bound to each other,
In holy marriage.

DON CARLO

Ah, do not be afraid. Have courage.

ELIZABETH

If I tremble still, it is not with fear.
I already feel reborn!
My soul surrenders
To a joy which is new to me.

DON CARLO

Do not be afraid! Take heart!
Oh, lovely betrothed!
Angel of love, raise your
Beloved eyes to me!

ELIZABETH AND DON CARLO

Intoxicated with love,
Let us swear again
The vow which united us;
Our lips spoke the vow;
Heaven is our witness;
Our hearts shaped the vow!
(*Tebaldo enters with Pages, carrying
    torches. The Pages remain behind, as
    Tebaldo advances toward Elizabeth.*)

TEBALDO

(*He kneels before her and kisses the hem
    of her gown.*)
To your loyal page, who now comes,
Oh, Signora, to bring joyous news,
I pray you grant this favor;
Keep me beside you forever.

ELIZABETH

(*She makes a sign for him to rise.*)
So be it!

TEBALDO

Oh, Queen, I salute you, the bride of
    King Philip.

ELISABETTA

(*tremante*)

No, no! sono all'infante dal padre
fiidanzata.


TEBALDO

Al monarca spagnuol v'ha Enrico
destinata!
Siete Regina.


ELISABETTA

Ahimè!


DON CARLO

(*tra sè*)

(Nel cor mi corse un gel!
L'abisso s'apre a me!
E tu lo soffri, o ciel!)


ELISABETTA

L'ora fatale è suonata!
Contro la sorte spietata
Crudo fia meno il pugnar.
Per sottrarmi a tanta pena
Per fuggir la ria catena,
Fin la morte io vò sfidar.


DON CARLO

L'ora fatale è suonata!
M'era la vita beata;
Cruda, funesta ora m'appar.
Di dolor quest'alma è piena,
Ah! dovrò la mia catena
In eterno dovrò trascinar.


CORO

(*Interno lontanissimo, che s'avvicina
a poco a poco.*)

Inni di festa lieti echeggiate,
E salutate il lieto dì . . .
La pace appresta felici istanti:
Due cori amanti il cielo unì!
Gloria ed onore alla più bella,
Onor a quella che dè doman,
Assisa in soglio gentil compagna,
Al Re di Spagna dar la sua man.


ELISABETTA

Tutto sparve . . .


DON CARLO

Sorte ingrata!


ELISABETTA

Al dolor son condannata!


DON CARLO

Spariva il sogno d'or,


ELISABETTA

Svaniva dal mio cor! Ah!
Svanì, ah! svaniva dal cor!


DON CARLO

Svaniva dal cor!


ELISABETTA

Ahimè! Ahimè!
Nostr'alma è condannata,
Non troverem mai più
Tanto amor, tanto ben.


CONTE DI LERMA

(*Ad* ELISABETTA)

Il glorioso Re di Francia, il grande
Enrico,
Al monarca di Spagna e dell'India
Vuol dar la man d'Isabella la sua
figliuola.
Questo vincol sarà suggello d'amistà,
Ma Filippo lasciarvi libertade vuol
intera;
Gradite voi la man del mio Re . . .
che la spera?


CORO DI DONNE

Accettate, Isabella, la man che vi
offre il Re: pietà! pietà!
La pace avrem alfin! pietà di noi!


CONTE DI LERMA

Che rispondete?


ELISABETTA

(*con voce morente*)

Sì.

(*Tra sè*)

(È l'angoscia suprema! Mi sento morir.)


DON CARLO

(Mi sento morir.)

**ELIZABETH**

No! No!
(*trembling*)
My father has betrothed me to the
  King's son!

**TEBALDO**

Henry has promised you to the King
  of Spain.
You are a Queen!

**ELIZABETH**

Alas!

**DON CARLO** (*to himself*)

A chill has pierced my heart!
Before me, an abyss opens; and you
  allow this to happen, oh, Heaven!

**ELIZABETH**

The fatal hour has come!
Against pitiless fate,
It is useless to fight.
To be spared such pain,
To be released from this wretched
  chain,
I will defy death itself!

**DON CARLO**

The fatal hour has come!
My life was joyous;
But now all seems cruel and disastrous
  to me.
My soul is filled with grief,
Ah! Shall I always have to drag
  with me
Sorrow's wretched chain?

**CHORUS**

(*from afar, gradually drawing nearer*)
Joyful hymns happily burst forth,
To greet this happy day!
Peace brings moments of joy;
Two loving hearts
Are joined as one!
Glory and honor to the most beautiful
  of all women,
To that woman who
Tomorrow will be seated on the throne,
Gentle companion to the King of Spain,
To whom she'll give her hand!

**ELIZABETH**

Everything is lost!

**DON CARLO**

Wretched fate!

**ELIZABETH**

I am condemned to grieve.

**DON CARLO**

Our golden dream disappeared . . .

**ELIZABETH**

Vanished, vanished, vanished . . .
From my heart!

**DON CARLO**

Vanished from my heart!

**ELIZABETH**

Alas! Alas!
Our souls are damned,
We will never find such love again, nor
  such joy.

**COUNT LERMA**
(*to Elizabeth*)

Great Henry, glorious King of France,
Wishes to give the hand of his daughter
  Isabella
To the ruler of Spain and India.
This bond will seal their friendship.
But Philip wishes to let you be wholly
  free.
Will you accept the hand of my King,
  who desires this?

**CHORUS OF WOMEN**

Isabella, accept the hand offered by
  the King: Pity! Pity!
At last we shall have peace!

**COUNT LERMA**

What is your answer?

**ELIZABETH** (*faintly*)

Yes.
(*To herself*)
This is the end, the last agony!

**DON CARLO**

I feel that I will die.

#### CORO

Vi benedica Iddio dal ciel!
La sorte amica vi sia fedel!
Inni di festa lieti echeggiate,
E salutate il lieto dì . . .
La pace appresta felici istanti;
Due cori amanti il cielo unì!

#### ELISABETTA

O dolor! O martir!
Nostr'alme condannate
Non Troveran mai più
Tanto amor.

#### DON CARLO

(tra sè)

(Mi sento morir. È l'angoscia suprema!)
Nostr'alme è condannate,
Tanto amor ora finì.

#### CORO

Regina Ispana,
Gloria, onor!
Gloria, Regina!

#### DON CARLO

Sparì un sogno così bel!
O destin fatal,
O destin crudel!

(ELISABETTA condotta dal CONTE di
LERMA entra nella lettiga. Il corteggio si mette in cammino. DON CARLO
rimane solo e desolato.)

## ATTO SECONDO

### SCENA 1

Il Chiostro del Convento di San Giusto.
Una cappella illuminata. Vi si vede
attraverso ad un cancello dorato la
tomba di Carlo V. A. destra, porta che
conduce all'esterno. In fondo la porta
interna del Chiostro. È l'alba.

#### CORO DI FRATI

(Nella capella)

Carlo il sommo Imperatore
Non è più che muta cener:
Del celeste suo fattore
L'alma altera or trema al piè.

#### UN FRATE

(Prostrato innanzi alla tomba, prega
sottovoce)

Ei voleva regnare sul mondo,
Obbliando Colui che nel ciel
Segna agli astri il cammino fedel.
L'orgolio immenso fu, fu l'error suo
      profondo!
Grand'è Dio sol, e s'Ei lo vuole
Fa tremar la terra ed il ciel!
Padre che arridi à tuoi fedel,
Pietoso al peccator
Conceder tu vorrai che la pace
E il perdon scendan dal ciel.
Grande è Dio sol! È grande Ei sol!

#### DON CARLO

Al chiostro di San Giusto
Ove finì la vita l'avo mio Carlo Quinto
Stanco di gloria e onor,
La pace cerco invan che tanto ambisce il
      cor.
Di lei che m'han rapita
L'imago erra con me del chiostro nel
      orror.

#### IL FRATE

(Avvicinandosi a Don Carlo)

Il duolo della terra
Nel chiostro ancor c'insegue
Del core sol la guerra
In ciel si calmerà!

#### DON CARLO

(Indietreggia spaventato)

La sua voce! Il cor mi trema!
Mi pareva . . . qual terror!
Veder l'Imperator che nelle lane
Il serto asconde e la lorica d'ôr.

(cupo)

È voce che nel chiostro appaia ancor!

#### IL FRATE

(Nell'interno sempre più allontanandosi)
Del core la guerra in ciel si calmerà!

#### DON CARLO

O terror! o terror!

## CHORUS

May God bless you!
From Heaven above!
May good fortune always be yours!
Echo, joyous hymns of celebration,
Salute this happy day,
Peace brings happy moments:
Two loving hearts are joined as one!

## ELIZABETH

Oh, suffering! Oh, sorrow!
Our souls are damned,
Never to love like this again!

## DON CARLO (to himself)

I think I shall die
No grief more cruel than this!
Our souls are damned
Never to love like this again!

## CHORUS

Oh, Queen of Spain,
Glory, honor!
Glory to the Queen!

## DON CARLO

Such a beautiful dream of love
    disappeared!
Oh, fatal destiny!
Oh, cruel destiny!

(Elizabeth, led by Count Lerma, goes to
    her litter. The court begins to leave.
    Don Carlo remains alone and deso-
    late.)

## ACT TWO

### SCENE 1

(The Convent of St. Just, in Spain. An
    illuminated chapel. Through a grille
    the tomb of the emperor Charles V
    can be seen. A door leads outside. At
    the rear, there is the door of the
    Cloister. Dawn.)

## CHORUS OF FRIARS
(in the chapel)

Charles, the mighty Emperor,
Is now nothing but ashes;
His proud heart trembles, humbled
Before his Divine Maker.

## A FRIAR

(prostrate before the tomb, praying in a
    low voice)

He wished to rule the world,
Forgetting God, who in heaven
Shows the stars their true way.
Immense was his pride; his error
    profound.
God alone is great; and if he so desires,
He shakes both heaven and earth!
Great God is good.
He takes pity on the sinner,
To sorrowing spirits He brings peace,
    and the pardon which comes from
    Him.
God alone is great! He alone is mighty!

## DON CARLO

Here is the cloister of St. Just,
Where Charles V, my ancestor, died,
    tired of glory and honors,
I vainly seek that peace which my
    heart desires.
The image of the woman whom they
    have torn from me
Follows me in horror to the cloister.

## FRIAR
(drawing near to Don Carlo)

Earthly misery
Follows us even into the cloister;
The strife that tears apart our hearts
Shall be laid to rest only in Heaven!

## DON CARLO
(draws back, frightened)

It is his voice! My heart trembles!
I thought that . . . What terror!
To see the Emperor, who hides in his
    woollen robes
His crown and golden cuirass.
(darkly)
This is the voice which still echoes in the
    cloister!

## FRIAR

(from within, farther and farther away)
The heart's strife shall be laid to rest in
    Heaven!

## DON CARLO

O terror! O terror!

(*Rodrigo entra.*)

RODRIGO

È lui! . . . desso! . . . l'Infante!

DON CARLO

O mio Rodrigo!

RODRIGO

Altezza!

DON CARLO

Sei tu, ch'io stringo al seno?

RODRIGO

O mio prence, signor!

DON CARLO

È il ciel che a me t'invia nel mio dolor,
Angiol consolator!

RODRIGO

L'ora suonò; te chiama il popolo
fiammingo!
Soccorrer tu lo dêi; ti fa suo salvator!
Ma che vid' io! quale pallor, qual
pena!
Un lampo di dolor sul ciglio tuo ba-
lena!
Muto sei tu! sospiri! hai tristo il cor!

(*Con trasporto d'affetto*)

Carlo mio, con me dividi il tuo pianto,
il tuo dolor!

DON CARLO

Mio salvator, mio fratel, mio fedele,
Lascia ch'io pianga in seno a te!

RODRIGO

Versami in cor il tuo strazio crudele,
L'anima tua non sia chiusa per me!
Parla!

DON CARLO

Lo vuoi tu? La mia sventura apprendi
E qual orrendo stral il mio cor tra-
passò!
Amo . . . d'un colpevol amor . . .
Elisabetta!

RODRIGO

Tua madre! Giusto ciel!

DON CARLO

Qual pallor! Lo sguardo chini al suol!
(*Con disperazione*)
Tristo me! tu stesso, mio Rodrigo,
T'allontani da me?

RODRIGO

No, Rodrigo ancor t'ama!
Io tel posso giurar.
Tu soffri? Già per me l'universo
dispar!

DON CARLO

O mio Rodrigo!

RODRIGO

Mio prence! Questo arcano dal Re
non fu sorpreso ancora?

DON CARLO

No!

RODRIGO

Ottien dunque da lui di partir per la
Fiandra.
Taccia il tuo cor; degna di te opra
farai,
Apprendi omai in mezzo a gente
oppressa
A divenir un Re!

DON CARLO

Ti seguirò, fratello.
(*Odesi il suono d'una campana*)

RODRIGO

Ascolta! Le porte dell'asil s'apron già;
Qui verranno Filippo e la Regina.

DON CARLO

Elisabetta!

RODRIGO

Rinfranca accanto a me lo spirto che
vacilla,
Serena ancora la stella tua nei cieli
brilla!
Domanda al ciel dei forti la virtù!

DON CARLO E RODRIGO

Dio, che nell'alma infondere
Amor volesti e speme,
Desio nel cor accendere
Tu dêi di libertà.
Giuriamo insiem di vivere
E di morire insieme;
In terra, in ciel congiungere
Ci può la tua bontà. Ah!
Dio, che nell'alma infondere
Amor volesti e speme,
Desio nel cor accendere
Tu dêi di libertà.

RODRIGO (*entering*)
'Tis he, Carlo . . . the prince!

DON CARLO
Oh, my Rodrigo!

RODRIGO
Your Highness!

DON CARLO
'Tis you, my friend Rodrigo!

RODRIGO
Ah, your Highness! My Lord!

DON CARLO
From Heaven you are sent
To cheer my heart,
Angel of hope and light.

RODRIGO
My friend, my Carlo!
The day has come. The people of
Flanders call Don Carlo,
In sacred duty bound,
Your brow in glory crowned.
But why this mien,
Speaking of dark depression?
Of gloom and bitter pain
It bears a grave expression.
You do not speak . . .
You're sighing . . . sad is your heart . . .
(*with sudden emotion*)
Oh my Carlo, my friend,
Let me share your grief,
Share your sadness,
Your sighs, your tears!

DON CARLO
You who have oft in the past
Been the stronger,
Share my dismay and my hopeless
despair!

RODRIGO
Open your heart!
Do not hide any longer
Sorrow and pain that your friend wants
to share!
Tell me . . .

DON CARLO
Can I dare?
Then hear my frightful secret
And tremble for my heart
Which no balm can restore:
I love—though in sinful despair—
Elizabeth!

RODRIGO
Your mother! God above!

DON CARLO
You are stunned . . .
Your eyes betray your reproach . . .
'Tis the end! I shall lose you forever.
My Rodrigo, must you cast me away?

RODRIGO
No. Rodrigo still loves you,
And united we are, I swear it
By the light of the sun and the stars.

DON CARLO
Oh, my Rodrigo!

RODRIGO
Has the King ever had a reason to
suspect you

DON CARLO
No.

RODRIGO
Then demand that he send you to
Flanders tomorrow!
Curb your desire!
Think of the task which you will find!
Among your people held in bondage
You will learn how to become a king.

DON CARLO
This I shall do, Rodrigo.
(*A bell is heard.*)

RODRIGO
Be careful!
The portals of the chapel will be
opened,
And King Philip will enter with the
Queen.

DON CARLO
Elizabeth!

RODRIGO
Take heart, my Prince,
Dispel the clouds of grief and sorrow.
Your rising star shines
So clear and bright upon tomorrow.
Have faith and pray
That God may be with you!

DON CARLO AND RODRIGO
He in His infinite love
Has filled the heart of man with fire,
Yes, God, our Lord, guiding us from
above,
Let freedom be our first desire.
Father in Heaven, steel our hearts,
Beating forever united!
To fight for right
Through death and night
Shall be our last, eternal plea! Ah!
Yes, God, our Lord, guiding us from
above,
Has meant us to be free!

RODRIGO

Vengon già.

DON CARLO

Oh terror! Al sol vederla io tremo!

RODRIGO

Coraggio!

(*Rodrigo s'è allontanato da Don Carlo che s'inchina innanzi al Re cupo e sospettoso. Egli cerca di frenar la sua emozione. Elisabetta trasale nel riveder Don Carlo. Il Re e la Regina si avanzano, e vanno verso la cappella ov'è la tomba di Carlo V, dinanzi alla quale Filippo s'inginocchia per un istante a capo scoperto; quindi prosegue il suo cammino colla Regina.*)

CORO DI FRATI (*Nell'interno*)

Carlo il sommo Imperatore
Non è più che muta cener,
Del celeste suo fattore
L'alma altera or trema al piè.
Grand'è Dio sol.

DON CARLO

Ei la fè sua! Io l'ho perduta;
Ah! gran Dio!

RODRIGO

Vien presso a me, il tuo cor più forte
avrai!

IL FRATE

Ah! La pace, il perdon discendono dal
cìel.
Grand' è Dio sol!

DON CARLO E RODRIGO

Vivremo insiem e morremo insiem!
Sarà l'estremo anelito,
Sarà un grido: Libertà!

SCENA 2

*I giardini alle porte del chiostro di S. Giusto. Una fontana; sedili di zolle; gruppi d'alberi d'aranci. All'orizzonte le montagne azzurre dell'Estremadura. In fondo a destra la porta del Convento.*

(*La Principessa d'Eboli, Tebaldo, la Contessa d'Aremberg, Dame della Regina, Paggi. Le Dame sono assise sulle zolle intorno a la fonte. Un paggio tempra una mandolina.*)

CORO DI DAME

Sotto ai folti, immensi abeti,
Che fan d'ombre e di quieti
Mite schermo al sacro ostel,
Ripariamo e a noi ristori
Dien i rezzi ai vivi ardori,
Che su noi dardeggia il ciel!

TEBALDO

Di mille fior si copre il suolo,
Dei pini s'ode il susurrar,
E sotto l'ombra aprir il vol
Qui l'usignuol più lieto par.

TEBALDO E CORO

Bello è udire in fra le piante
Mormorar la fonte amante,
Stilla a stilla, i suoi dolor!
E, se il sole é piu cocente,
Le ore far del dì men lente
Infra l'ombra e in mezzo ai fior.

EBOLI

Tra queste mura pie la Regina di
Spagna
Può sola penetrar.
Volete voi, mie compagne, già che le
stelle in ciel
Spuntate ancor non son, cantar
qualche canzon?

CORO

Seguir vogliam il tuo capriccio,
O principessa, attente udrem.

EBOLI (*a Tebaldo*)

A me recate la mandolina:
E cantiam tutte insiem,
Cantiam la canzon saracina,
Quella del Velo, proprizia all'amor.
Cantiam!

TEBALDO E CORO

Cantiam!

EBOLI

(*Il Paggio l'accompagna sulla mandolina.*)

Nei giardin del bello saracin ostello
All'olezzo, al rezzo degli allôr, dei fior
Una bell'almea, tutta chiusa in vel,
Contemplar parea una stella in ciel.

**RODRIGO**

They are here!

**DON CARLO**

Stay with me!
I cannot bear to see her.

**RODRIGO**

Be careful!

(*King Philip and the Queen enter in
the midst of a group of monks. Rodrigo withdraws from Carlo who bows
before the King who appears somber
and suspicious. Carlo tries to hide
his feelings while Elizabeth is visibly
flustered when she sees him. King
and Queen step to the tomb of
Charles V, where Philip genuflects
and bares his head. They then proceed on their way.*)

**CHORUS OF MONKS**

(*from offstage*)

Proud and mighty in his splendor,
Now returned to dust and ashes,
Charles the Fifth refused to render
Unto God his haughty heart.
Thine is the pow'r, almighty God.

**DON CARLO**

She is his wife! And I have lost her!
Ah, my God!

**RODRIGO**

Come here to me and steel your
    courage, steel your heart!

**THE FRIAR**

Ah, I pray for forgivenesss,
Father and Lord.
Thine is the glory, Thine alone.

**DON CARLO AND RODRIGO**

I stand with you
Until Death do us part,
Throughout our life to fight for right,
Till men can shout in joyous glee:
We are free!

**SCENE 2**

In the garden adjoining the Monastery
    of St. Just. A fountain surrounded
    by grass-covered mounds and orange-
    trees. On the horizon the blue moun-
    tains of Estremadura. Upstage right
    the door of the monastery.

(*The Princess of 'Eboli, Tebaldo, the
Countess of Aremberg and other
ladies-in-waiting, pages, etc. The
ladies are sitting on the grassy
mounds around the fountain, the
pages at their feet. One of the pages
is tuning a mandolin.*)

**CHORUS OF LADIES**

Gentle shadows so cool and tender
Of these pines in their friendly
    splendor,
Pious guardians of blissful calm,
May you still our impatient yearning
For relief from the sunrays burning,
As we drink of your fragrant balm.

**TEBALDO**

A thousand flowers all around us
Sway lightly in the lazy air,
As in the branches the little birds
Are sprightly singing everywhere.

**LADIES AND TEBALDO**

Over there in lively dances,
Whispering passionate romances,
Springs a fountain so clear and cool.
While the grove lends us protection
We can enjoy the sweet reflection
Of the blossoms in the silv'ry pool.

**EBOLI**

Beyond these holy portals
In solitary worship
The Queen has gone to pray.
Let us enjoy, while we are waiting,
The magic in the air,
And praise the florid bounty
In music and in song!

**CHORUS**

We are with you. We want to hear you.
We'll pay attention, eye and ear.

**EBOLI** (*to Tebaldo*)

You'll play the mandolin, I pray you,
And you join in the song,
The song of the Reticent Beauty . . .
Surely you know it . . .
The Song of the Veil! Let's sing!

**LADIES AND TEBALDO**

Go on!

(*Eboli sings, accompanied by Tebaldo.*)

**EBOLI**

Night's enchanting splendor
Bade the world surrender.
Silent fell the vendor,
Still the streets below,

Mohammed, Re moro, al giardin sen
va;
Dice a lei: t'adoro, o gentil beltà . . .
Vien, a sè t'invita per regnare il Re;
La Regina ambita non è più da me.
Ah!

EBOLI, TEBALDO E CORO

Ah! Tessete i veli,
Vaghe donzelle,
Mentre è nei cieli
L'astro maggior,
Chè sono i veli,
Al brillar delle stelle,
Più cari all'amor.

EBOLI

Ma discerno appena,
(Chiaro il ciel non è)
I capelli belli,
La man breve, il piè . . .
Deh! solleva il velo
Che t'asconde a me;
Esser come il cielo
Senza vel tu dè.
Se il tuo cor vorrai
A me dare in don,
Il mio trono avrai
Chè sovrano io son.

(Parlato)

Tu lo vuoi? t'inchina,
Appagar ti vo.
"Allah! La Regina!" Mohammed
sclamò. Ah! Ah!

EBOLI, TEBALDO E CORO

Tessete i veli,
Vaghe donzelle,
Mentre è nei cieli
L'astro maggior,
Chè sono i veli,
Al brillar delle stelle,
Più cari all'amor.

(Elisabetta esce dal Convento.)

CORO DI DONNE

La Regina!

EBOLI (Tra sè)

(Un'arcana mestizia sul suo core pesa
ognora.)

ELISABETTA

(Sedendo presso il fonte)

Una canzon qui lieta risuonò. (Tra sè)
(Ahimè! spariro i dì che lieto era il
mio cor!)
(Rodrigo appare nel fondo. Tebaldo
s'avanza verso di lui, gli parla un
momento a voce bassa, poi torna alla
Regina, presentando Rodrigo.)

TEBALDO

Il marchese di Posa, Grande di
Spagna.

RODRIGO

(Inchinandosi alla Regina)

Signora! Per Vostra Maestà, l'augusta
madre
Un foglio mi confidò in Parigi.
(Rodrigo porge la lettera alla Regina,
e rapidamente le consegna un biglie-
tto; quindi mostra alle dame il real
foglio.)
(Leggete, in nome della grazia eterna.)
Ecco il regal suggel,
I fiordalisi d'ôr.

(Elisabetta rimane un momento immobile e confusa, mentre Rodrigo
s'avvicina ad Eboli.)

EBOLI

(A mezza voce a Rodrigo)

Che mai si fa nel suol francese, così
gentil, cosi cortese?

RODRIGO (ad Eboli)

D'un gran torneo si parla già,
E del torneo il Re sarà.

ELISABETTA

(Tenendo in mano il biglietto)

Ah! non ardisco aprirlo ancor;
Se il fo, tradisco del Re l'onor.

EBOLI (a Rodrigo)

Son le Francesi gentili tanto, e d'ele-
ganza,
Di grazia han vanto.

ELISABETTA

Ah! perchè tremo!

RODRIGO (ad Eboli)

In voi brillar sol si vedrà la grazia insieme alla beltà.

EBOLI (a Rodrigo)

È mai ver ch'alle feste regali
Le Francesi hanno tali beltà,
Che solo in ciel trovan rivali?

ELISABETTA

Quest'alma è pura ancora.
Dio mi legge in cor.

As the Moorish beauty
Kissed the moon so pale,
Mindful of her duty,
Through her silken veil.
Came the King, so handsome,
So strong and tall.
"What will be your ransom?"
The King would call.
"Come, my pretty maiden,
It is you I adore,
For the Queen is fading
And a terrible bore!" Ah!

ALL
Slyly in hiding, never confiding,
Coyly deciding how much to show,
Caution be guiding firmly our heart,
Till we show that we know where we go!

EBOLI
"Let the moon behold you
In his silver-glow!
For my eyes have told you
That I love you so!
Come, remove the veil
Which hides your face so fair,
You, whose charms so frail
Cause even stars to stare.
Let your heart be mine
For the rest of my life!
Make my nights divine
As my lovely young wife!"
"If you wish, come nearer!
Your reward I bring."
"Oh no! Allah help me!
'Tis the Queen!" said the King. Ah!

ALL
Slyly in hiding, never confiding,
Coyly deciding how much to show,
Caution be guiding firmly our heart,
Till we show that we know where we go!
(*The Queen comes out of the monastery.*)

LADIES' CHORUS
The Queen!

EBOLI (*aside*)
(A mysterious sadness
Holds her heart forever in bondage.)

ELIZABETH
Happy and gay, you sang a merry song.
(*aside*)
(For me the days of joy
Will not return again.)

(*Rodrigo appears in the background. Tebaldo approaches him. After a brief exchange of words, the page turns to the Queen to introduce Rodrigo.*)

TEBALDO
Don Rodrigo de Posa, Grandee of Spain.

RODRIGO
(*bowing to the Queen*)
Her Majesty, the Queen, your noble mother,
Has asked me to bring you this from Paris.
(*Rodrigo, while handing the letter to the Queen, quickly slips her a note, then shows the Ladies the royal crest on the letter. He whispers to the Queen.*)
Read it, in the name of our Holy Virgin!
(*in a normal voice*)
The royal seal of France,
A lily wrought in gold.
(*For a moment, Elizabeth remains motionless and confused while Rodrigo turns to Eboli.*)

EBOLI
(*in a conversational tone, to Rodrigo*)
And how is life across the border,
In France, the home of law and order?

RODRIGO (*to Eboli*)
A tournament thrills every heart.
They say the King himself announced
He will take part.

ELIZABETH
(*holding the note in her hand*)
(I do not dare it, to read it here!
How can I bear it, this dreadful fear!)

EBOLI (*to Rodrigo*)
And are the Frenchmen as they claim to be,
So strong and courteous
As all the Spaniards aim to be?

ELIZABETH
(Heart, do not tremble!)

RODRIGO (*to Eboli*)
In you indeed Nature has combined
Both beauty and brilliance of the mind.

EBOLI (*to Rodrigo*)
Is it true that at dinners and dances
There in France you see beauties so fair
That even angels could not hide their glances?

ELIZABETH
(My heart is blameless,
It still is blameless.
Heaven knows my heart.)

RODRIGO (*ad Eboli*)
La più bella mancar lor potrà.

EBOLI (*a Rodrigo*)
Dite è ver?
Nei balli a Corte, pei nostri manti la
seta
E l'ôr sono eleganti?

ELISABETTA
(*A parte, leggendo il biglietto*)
(Per la memoria che ci lega,
In nome d'un passato a me caro,
V'affidate a costui, ven prego—Carlo.)

RODRIGO (*ad Eboli*)
Tutto sta ben allor che s'ha
La vostra grazia e la beltà.

ELISABETTA (*a Rodrigo*)
Grata io son. Un favor chiedete alla
Regina.

RODRIGO (*Vivamente*)
Accetto, e non per me.

ELISABETTA (*Tra sè*)
(Io mi sostengo appena!)

EBOLI (*a Rodrigo*)
Chi più degno di voi può sue brame
veder appagate?

ELISABETTA (*Tra sè*)
(Oh terror!)

EBOLI
Ditelo, chi?

ELISABETTA
Chi mai?

RODRIGO
Carlo ch'è sol il nostro amore
Vive nel duol su questo suol,
E nessun sa quanto dolore
Del suo bel cor fa vizzo il fior.
In voi la speme è di chi geme;
S'abbia la pace ed il vigor;
Dato gli sia che vi riveda,
Se tornerà, salvo sarà.

EBOLI (*Tra sè*)
(Un dì che presso a sua madre mi
stava
Vidi Carlo tremar . . .)

ELISABETTA (*Tra sè*)
(La doglia in me s'aggrava
Rivederlo è morir!)

EBOLI (*Tra sè*)
(Amor avria, avria per me?
Perchè lo cela a me?)

RODRIGO
Ah! Carlo del Re suo genitore
Rinchiuso il cor ognor trovò;
Eppur non so chi dell'amore
Saria più degno, ah! inver nol so.
Un sol, un solo detto d'amore
Sparir il duolo farà dal cor;
Dato gli sia che vi riveda,
Se tornerà, se tornerà, salvo sarà.

ELISABETTA (*Tra sè*)
(Ahimè! io mi sostengo appena!
Gran Dio! Rivederlo è morir!)

EBOLI (*Tra sè*)
(Amor avria, amor avria, avria per me?
Perchè lo cela, perchè celarlo a me?)

ELISABETTA
(*A Tebaldo con dignità e risoluzione*)
Va, pronta io son il figlio a riveder.

EBOLI (*Fra sè agitata*)
(Oserà mai, oserà mai?
Potesse aprirmi, aprirmi il cor!)
(*Rodrigo prende la mano d'Eboli e
s'allontana con lei parlando sotto-
voce*)
(*Don Carlo si mostra condotto da
Tebaldo. Rodrigo parla sommesso a
Tebaldo che entra nel Convento.
Don Carlo s'avvicina lentamente ad
Elisabetta e s'inchina senza alzar lo
sguardo su di lei. Elisabetta con-
tenendo a fatica la sua emozione,
ordina a Don Carlo d'avvicinarsi.*)
*Rodrigo ed Eboli scambiano dei cenni
con le Dame, si allontanano e finiscono per disperdersi tra gli alberi.
La Contessa d' Aremberg e le due
Dame restano sole in piedi, a distan-
za, impacciate del contegno che deb-
bono avere. A poco a poco la Contessa e le Dame vanno di cespuglio
in cespuglio cogliendo qualche fiore,
e si allontanano.*)

RODRIGO (*to Eboli*)
One more beautiful than they
Will yet go there!

EBOLI (*to Rodrigo*)
Is this true? But did you notice
A diff'rence in their bearing?
How do they look?
What are they wearing?

ELIZABETH
(*aside, reading the note*)
("By the remembrances that bind
  us, by what is past and gone
  but not forgotten, I beseech
  you to trust the bearer. Carlo.")

RODRIGO (*to Eboli*)
How could I say? All I can tell:
(*with a bow to Eboli*)
I never met a fairer demoiselle!

ELIZABETH (*to Rodrigo*)
Thank you, Marquis! Do you wish
To ask the Queen a favor?

RODRIGO (*eagerly*)
I do, but not for me.

ELIZABETH (*aside*)
(God grant me strength to hear it!)

EBOLI (*to Rodrigo*)
Not for you, Marquis?
Who then is worthy to seek a royal
  favor?

ELIZABETH (*aside*)
(Lord above!)

EBOLI
Who could it be?

ELIZABETH
Yes, who?

RODRIGO
Carlo, your son, restless and haunted,
He has come here in hope and fear.
He, once so brave, strong and un-
  daunted,
Now seems forlorn, depressed, and torn.
You are the hope that will aid and sus-
  tain him,
You can restore him to life once more!
Grant his desire once more to see you!
Grant it, my Queen, and he shall find
His smile again!

EBOLI (*aside*)
(One day when near me the Queen
  spoke to Carlo. He was trembling
  and pale . . .)

ELIZABETH (*aside*)
(How can I bear this torment?
To be near him is to die!)

EBOLI (*aside*)
(Could it be true? Could he love me?
Why does he hide his heart?)

RODRIGO
Ah! Carlo in vain sought from his
  father
Guidance and hope in his despair.
Yet, in this world no one should rather
Proudly be loved as a son and heir.
One single gesture of love and affection
Will banish sorrow from Carlo' s heart.
Grant his desire once more to see you,
Grant it, my Queen, and he shall find
His smile again!

ELIZABETH (*aside*)
(The Lord may grant me courage to
  see him!
Oh God! To be near him is to die!)

EBOLI (*aside*)
(Don Carlo here? My love so near?
Why is he silent?
What could he have to fear?)

ELIZABETH
(*to Tebaldo, with dignity and firmness*)

Go! I am prepared to see my son.

EBOLI (*aside, nervously*)
(Why is he here? Oh hope, oh fear!
Could Carlo love me? What does he
  fear?)

(*Rodrigo offers his arm to Eboli and,
conversing softly, leads her off.*)

(*Don Carlo is admitted by Tebaldo.
Rodrigo quietly gives some instructions to Tebaldo who subsequently
disappears into the monastery. Don
Carlo slowly advances towards the
Queen and bows to her without ever
raising his eyes. Barely able to control her emotions, the Queen beckons
him to come closer. Rodrigo and
Eboli motion the ladies to disperse
slowly among the trees. The Countess
of Aremberg and two of the ladies
stay nearby, somewhat unsure of
what they should do. After a while
they, too, pretending to gather flowers, withdraw gracefully.*)

DON CARLO (*Con calma*)

Io vengo a domandar grazia alla mia
    Regina;
Quella che in cor del Re tiene il posto
    primero
Sola potrà ottener questa grazia per
    me.

(*Animandosi a poco a poco*)

Quest'aura m'è fatale, m'opprime, mi
    tortura,
Come il pensier d'una sventura.
Ch'io parta! n'è mestier!
Andar mi faccia il Re nelle Fiandre.

ELISABETTA (*Commossa*)

Mio figlio!

DON CARLO (*Con veemenza*)

Tal nome no; ma quel d'altra volta!

(*Elisabetta vuole allontanarsi. Don
Carlo supplichevole l'arresta.*)

Infelice! più non reggo!
Pietà! soffersi tanto; pietà!
Il ciel avaro un giorno sol mi diè,
Poi rapillo a me!

(*Rodrigo ed Eboli attraversano la
scena conversando.*)

ELISABETTA

Prence, se vuol Filippo udire la mia
    preghiera,
Per la Fiandra da lui rimessa in vostra
    man
Ben voi potrete partir doman.

(*Rodrigo ed Eboli sono partiti. Elisabetta fa un cenna d'addio a Don
Carlo e vuole allontanarsi.*)

DON CARLO

Ciel! non un sol, un sol detto
Pel meschino ch'esul sen va!
Ah! perchè mai parlar non sento
Nel vostro cor la pietà?
Ahimè! quest'alma è oppressa,
Ho in core, ho in core un gel . . .
Insan! piansi, pregai nel mio delirio,
Mi volsi a un gelido marmo d'avel!

ELISABETTA (*molto commossa*)

Perchè accusar il cor d'indifferenza?
Capir dovreste questo nobil silenzio.
Il dover, come un raggio al guardo
    mio brillò;

Guidata da quel raggio io moverò
La speme pongo in Dio, nell'inno-
    cenza!

DON CARLO (*con voce morente*)

Perduto ben, mio sol tesor,
Ah! tu splendor di mia vita!
Udir almen ti poss'ancor.
Quest'alma ai detti tuoi schiuder si
    vede il ciel!

ELISABETTA

Clemente Iddio, così bel cor
Acqueti il suo duol nell'obblio . . .
O Carlo, addio; su questa terra
Vivendo accanto a te mi crederei nel
    ciel!

DON CARLO (*con esaltazione*)

O prodigio! Il mio cor s'affida, si
    consola;
Il sovvenir del dolor s'invola,
Il ciel pietà sentì di tanto duol.
Isabella, al tuo piè morir io vo' d'amor.

(*Don Carlo cade privo di sensi al
suolo.*)

ELISABETTA

Giusto ciel, la vita già manca
Nell'occhio suo che lagrimò!
Bontà celeste, deh! tu rinfranca
Quel nobil core che sì penò.
Ahimè! il dolor l'uccide
Tra queste braccia io lo vedrò
Morir d'affanno, morir d'amore,
Colui che il ciel mi destinò!

DON CARLO (*nel delirio*)

Qual voce a me dal ciel scende a
    parlar d'amor?
Elisabetta! tu, bell'adorata.

ELISABETTA

O delirio, o terror!

DON CARLO

Assisa accanto a me come ti vidi un dì!
Ah! il ciel s'illuminò, la selva rifiorì!

DON CARLO *(calmly)*
I've come to beg my Queen
For her gracious assistance,
Knowing that of the heart of the King
She is mistress.
No one could speak so well
For my humble request.
*(increasingly excited)*
Around here I am dying,
Am choking in frustration!
Send me away, away forever!
I beg you . . . I must leave.
The King shall send me on to Flanders.

ELIZABETH *(visibly moved)*
Oh, son!

DON CARLO *(vehemently)*
Ah, not that name!
The one I remember! . . .
*(Elizabeth is on the verge of leaving. Carlo holds her back, pleading.)*
You are leaving . . . you refuse me!
Forgive . . . how I suffer . . . forgive!
Why do the angels permit us to enjoy
What at last they destroy!
*(Absorbed in conversation, Rodrigo and Eboli cross the stage.)*

ELIZABETH
Highness, if my husband will agree
To my plea and your suggestion,
If he wishes for Flanders
To be in your command . . .
I see no reason why you should
Not be on your way at once.
*(Rodrigo and Eboli have left the stage. Elizabeth makes a gesture of farewell to Carlo and starts leaving.)*

DON CARLO
You . . . not a word? You dismiss me . . .
See no reason for me to stay?
Why in this final hour deny
My yearning for a sign of compassion?
Insane with suff'ring, and broken,
I need of your pity a token.
In vain I want to die, to end the torment,
The sorrow, the anguish
Which your cold heart defies.

ELIZABETH *(greatly moved)*
But why, why blame my heart
For coldness and indiff'rence,
When you must know what bids
My conscience be silent?

Like a ray sent from Heaven
My duty shines so bright:
It guide my haunted heart
To what is right, and God on high
Will help me try to find redemption.

DON CARLO
*(as if about to die)*
Sink down, oh night, fade out, you star!
My dream of love has ended!
Farewell, delight of days so far!
Now darkness has descended
Over my dying heart.

ELIZABETH
Oh Lord above, so great, so kind,
Thy mercy shall be granted
To him, whose love, whose noble mind
Have made my life enchanted
Until our ways must part!

DON CARLO
*(feverishly exalted)*
Oh wonder! My heart is peaceful and quiet.
My bitter grief, my despair have ended.
At last, at last the angels take pity on my soul!
Isabella, my love . . . oh joy to die with you!
*(He faints.)*

ELIZABETH
Oh Heaven, his life is in danger,
His breaking eyes are filled with tears!
Oh Holy Virgin, pray for him,
Who suffers past enduring!
His pain, his despair will kill him.
And in these arms I shall enfold,
At last in tender embrace to hold
The man whom God gave me to love! . . .

DON CARLO *(delirious)*
A voice from Heaven sent
Came down to sing of love;
My heart, to meet it, went
Up to the stars above . . .

ELIZABETH
I must listen no more!

DON CARLO
Entranced, my eyes can see
A dream of memory:
'Tis you, Elizabeth,
My radiant bride-to-be.

ELISABETTA

Egli muore! O ciel, ei muore!

DON CARLO

O mio tesor! sei tu, mio dolce amor!

ELISABETTA

Gran Dio! giusto ciel!

DON CARLO (*rinvenendo*)

Alla mia tomba, al sonno dell'avel
Sottrarmi perchè vuoi, spietato ciel!

ELISABETTA

Oh! Carlo! Oh! Carlo!

DON CARLO

Sotto al mio piè si dischiuda la terra
Il capo mio sia dal fulmin colpito,
Io t'amo, io t'amo, Elisabetta,

(*La stringe fra le braccia*)

Il mondo è a me sparito!

ELISABETTA (*scostandosi*)

Compi l'opra, a svenar corri il padre,
Ed allor del suo sangue macchiato,
All'altar puoi menare la madre . . .
Va . . . va . . . e svena tuo padre!

DON CARLO

(*Retrocedendo inorridito*)

Ah! maledetto io son!

(*Fugge disperato*)

ELISABETTA

Ah! Iddio su noi vegliò!

(*Cade in ginocchio*)

Signor! Signor!

(*Filippo II, Tebaldo, La Contessa
d'Aremberg, Rodrigo, Eboli, Coro,
Paggi entrando successivamente.*)

TEBALDO

(*Uscendo precipitosamente dal chiostro*)

Il Re!

FILIPPO (*Ad Elisabetta*)

Perchè sola è la Regina?
Non una dama almeno presso di voi
serbaste?
Nota non v'è la legge mia regal?
Quale dama d'onor esser dovea con
voi?

(*La Contessa d'Aremberg esce tremente dalla calca, e si presenta al Re.*)

(*Alla Contessa*)

Contessa, al nuovo sol in Francia
tornerete.

(*La Contessa d'Aremberg scoppia in
lagrime. Tutti guardano la Regina
con sorpresa.*)

CORO

Ah! La Regina egli offende!

ELISABETTA

Non pianger, mia compagna, non
pianger no,
Lenisci il tuo dolor.
Bandita sei di Spagna
Ma non da questo cor.
Non dir del pianto mio,
Del crudo mio dolor;
Ritorna al suol natio,
Ti seguirà il mio cor.

(*Dà un anello alla Contessa*)

Ricevi estremo pegno,
Un pegno di tutto il mio favor;
Cela l'oltraggio indegno
Onde arrossisco ancor.
Non dir del pianto mio,
Del crudo mio dolor;
Ritorna al suol natio,
Ti seguirà mio cor.

RODRIGO E CORO

Spirto gentil e pio
Acqueta il tuo dolor.

FILIPPO (*Tra sè*)

(Come al cospetto mio
Infinge un nobil cor!)

(*La Regina si separa piangendo dalla
Contessa ed esce sorreggendosi ad
Eboli. Il coro la segue.*)

ELIZABETH

He is dying! May Heaven save him!

DON CARLO

Now you are mine at last, yes,
For all eternity you are mine!

ELIZABETH

Ah! Heaven help me! Gracious Lord!

DON CARLO  (coming to)

Why bring me back to life,
Now that I saw an end
To pain and strife?

ELIZABETH

Oh Carlo! Oh Carlo!

DON CARLO

Open the way to eternal damnation!
Death and decay may destroy all cre-
ation!
I love you, I love you, Elizabeth,

(taking her in his arms)

And if the world must end,
I make you mine!

ELIZABETH

(breaking free)

Then go on to murder your father!
With his blood on your hands
To the altar,
With his blood on your hands,
To exalt her, to embrace as your wife
Your own mother . . . go! Go! Go!
Go, and kill your father!

DON CARLO

(reeling back, aghast)

Almighty God! No! No!

(He flees in utmost despair.)

ELIZABETH

God, the Lord has saved
Our hearts once more! Oh Lord! Oh
Lord!

(She sinks to her knees.)

(King Philip, Tebaldo, the Countess of
Aremberg, Rodrigo, Eboli, the ladies-
in-waiting, Philip's entourage, and
pages enter in quick succession.)

TEBALDO

(hurrying from the cloister)

The King!

PHILIP (to Elizabeth)

Why is the Queen alone?
Not one among your retinue
Attended to her duty?
Do you not know what royal law de-
mands?
Of your ladies-in-waiting,
Who should have been with you?

(The Countess of Aremberg steps out
of the group and approaches the
King, trembling.)

PHILIP (to the Countess)

My Countess, you return
To France without delay!

(The Countess breaks out in tears.
Everybody looks at the Queen, star-
tled.)

CHORUS (to themselves)

(Ah! 'Tis the Queen he has offended.)

ELIZABETH

These tears of pain and grieving,
Oh stem their flow
And dry their bitter dew!
Though Spain you will be leaving,
My heart will stay with you.
Together we were yearning
To hear the ancient chants:
Oh greet upon returning
The sunny sky of France!

(handing the Countess a ring)

Receive of my affection a token
Which only you shall wear!
My sadness and dejection
In silence I shall bear.
Conceal my grief and sorrow,
My pain, this cruel mischance:
Returning there tomorrow,
Oh greet the sky of France,
The sunny sky of my beloved France!

RODRIGO AND CHORUS

(Oh may her noble heart
To gladness be restored!)

PHILIP (aside)

(How in deceitful art
To lie she can afford!)

(In tears, the Queen moves away from
the Countess and leaves the scene,
supported by Eboli. Everybody withdraws, including Rodrigo, who is
ordered to remain by the King.)

FILIPPO

(*A Rodrigo che vuol uscire*)

Restate!

(*Rodrigo pone un ginocchio a terra;
poi s'avvicina al Re e si covre il
capo senz'alcun impaccio.*)

Presso alla mia persona
Perchè d'esser ammesso voi
Non chiedeste ancor?
Io so ricompensar
Tutti i miei difensor;
Voi serviste, lo so,
Fido alla mia corona.

RODRIGO

Sperar che mai potrei dal favore dei
Re?
Sire, pago son io, la legge è scudo a
me.

FILIPPO

Amo uno spirto altier.
L'audacia perdono . . . non sempre . . .
(*Pausa*)
Voi lasciaste il mestier della guerra;
Un uomo come voi, soldato d'alta
stirpe,
Inerte può restar?

RODRIGO

Ove alla Spagna una spada bisogni,
Una vindice man, un custode all'onor,
Bentosto brillerà la mia di sangue
intrisa!

FILIPPO

Ben lo so . . . ma per voi . . . che far
poss'io?

RODRIGO

Nulla! No . . . nulla per me! ma per
altri . . .

FILIPPO

Che vuoi dire? per altri?

RODRIGO

Io parlerò, Sire, se grave non v'è!

FILIPPO

Favella!

RODRIGO

O signor, di Fiandra arrivo,
Quel paese un dì sì bel:
D'ogni luce or fatto privo
Ispira orror, par muto avel!
L'orfanel che non ha loco
Per le vie piangendo va;
Tutto struggon ferro e foco,
Bandita è la pietà!

La riviera che rosseggia
Scorrer sangue al guardo par;
Della madre il grido echeggia
Pei figiuoli che spirâr!
Ah! sia benedetto Iddio,
Che narrar lascia a me
Questa cruda agonia
Perchè sia nota al Re.

FILIPPO

Col sangue sol potei la pace aver del
mondo.
Il brando mio calcò l'orgoglio ai novator,
Che illudono le genti coi sogni menti-
tor!
La morte in questa man ha un avvenir
fecondo.

RODRIGO

Che! Voi pensate seminando morte,
Piantar per gli anni eterni?

FILIPPO

Volgi un guardo alle Spagne!
L'artigian cittadin, la plebe alle cam-
pagne
A Dio fedel e al Re un lamento non
ha!
La pace istessa io dono alle mie Fiandre!

RODRIGO

Orrenda, orrenda pace! la pace è dei
sepolcri!
O Re! non abbia mai di voi l'istoria a
dir:
Ei fu Neron!
Quest'è la pace che voi date al mondo?
Desta tal don terror, orror profondo!
È un carnefice il prete, un bandito
ogni armier!
Il popol geme e si spegne tacendo,
È il vostro imper deserto immenso,
orrendo,
S'ode ognun a Filippo maledir, si,
maledir!
Come un Dio redentor, l'orbe inter
rinovate,
V'ergete a vol sublime, sovra d'ogn'
altro Re!
Per voi si allieti il mondo! date la
libertà.

PHILIP (*to Rodrigo*)
Remain here!

(*Rodrigo genuflects before the King, then goes towards him, without showing any sign of awe.*)

I noticed you around me.
Why have you never yet
Endeavored to speak to me?
I know how to reward
Those who fought for the crown.
I know well what you did
In the defense of Spain.

RODRIGO
A duty well performed
Needs no further reward.
Sire, I need no favors.
The law shall be my Lord.

PHILIP
You are a man of pride
And seem independent . . . be careful!

(*after a pause*)

You have lately resigned your commission.
How can a man like you,
A soldier to the core,
Enjoy a life of rest?

RODRIGO
Should once again
Spain have need of her servant,
Of a man who can fight,
Of a powerful sword:
Her glory shall find
My life at her command at once.

PHILIP
That I know.
But for now . . . what are you asking?

RODRIGO
Nothing . . . no! . . . Nothing for me . . .
But for others . . .

PHILIP
How surprising . . . for others?

RODRIGO
May I speak out, Sire? Do I have your consent?

PHILIP
Speak freely!

RODRIGO
I have come, oh Sire, from Flanders,
From that land once rich and fair;
Yet today everywhere one wanders
The stench of death is in the air.
Without food, naked and crying,
Little orphans will bar your path,
Swelling, with the cries of the dying,
The roaring storm of wrath!

From farm and home come flying
The hungry flames of war.
In vain a mother's sighing
For sons who are no more!
I praise eternal Heaven
For having brought me here, Sire,
To tell you the truth,
No matter how severe.

PHILIP
Terror will often serve
To keep the world contented.
In blood I had to drown
Rebellion on the rise,
Deluding people's minds
With its fallacies and lies.
Destruction, if wisely used,
Is counterpart to mercy.

RODRIGO
Sire, do you hold
That, if you sow destruction,
You reap a better future?

PHILIP
Look around you and tell me:
Is there one to complain?
In Spain, with all her people,
You find a happy land
Under God and the crown.
This is the kind of peace
I want for Flanders.

RODRIGO
A peace of death and silence!
Its symbol is the graveyard!
Sire, may never History once say of you:
He was a Nero!
What you have brought
You claim to be salvation.
What you have wrought instead
Has been damnation!
Sacred robes hide the hangman,
Helmets shield assassins' heads!
The people tremble and suffer in silence.
Throughout this vast
And seething reign of terror
Every mouth whispers curses
Against the King, yes,
Against the King!
Like a god, heaven-sent,
You could fashion
A world bright and splendent,
Greater than all
Who came before you,
Never to fade from the hearts of men:
Through you come true
The dream of liberty!
Oh set your people free!

**FILIPPO**

Oh! strano sognator!
Tu muterai pensier, se il cor dell'uom
Conoscerai, qual Filippo il conosce!
Or non più! Ha nulla inteso il Re . . .
Non temer! (*Cupo*)
Ma . . . ti guarda dal Grande Inquisi-
tor!

**RODRIGO**

Che! . . . Sire!

**FILIPPO**

Tu resti in mia regal presenza
E nulla ancora hai domandato al Re?
Io voglio averti a me d'accanto!

**RODRIGO**

Sir! No! Quel ch'io son restar io vo'!

**FILIPPO**

Sei troppo altier!
Osò lo sguardo tuo penetrar . . . il mio
soglio . . .
Del capo mio, che grava la corona,
L'angoscia apprendi e il duol!
Guarda or tu la mia reggia!
L'affanno . . . la circonda, sgraziato
genitor!
Sposo più triste ancor!

**RODRIGO**

Sire, che dite mai?

**FILIPPO**

La Regina . . . un sospetto mi turba
. . . mio figlio!

**RODRIGO** (*Con impeto*)

Fiera ha l'alma insieme pura!

**FILIPPO**

(*Con esplosione di dolore*)

Nulla val sotto al ciel
Il ben ch'ei tolse a me!
(*Rodrigo, spaventato, guarda Filippo,
senza rispondere.*)
Il lor destin affido a te!
Scruta quei cor, che un folle amor
trascina!
Sempre lecito è a te di scontrar la
Regina!
Tu, che sol sei un uom, fra lo stuol
uman,
Ripongo il cor nella leal tua man!

**RODRIGO**

(*A parte, con trasporto di gioia*)

(Inaspettata aurora in ciel appar!
S'aprì quel cor che niun potè
scrutar!)

**FILIPPO**

In tua man!
Possa cotanto dì la pace a me tornar!

**RODRIGO**

(Oh! sogno mio divin!
Oh! gloriosa speme!)

**FILIPPO** (*Cupo*)

Ti guarda dal Grande Inquisitor!
Ti guarda! Ti guarda!

**RODRIGO**

Sire!
(*Il Re stende la mano a Rodrigo, che
s'inginocchia e gliela bacia.*)
(*La tela cala rapidamente*)

# ATTO TERZO

### SCENA 1

*I Giardini della Regina a Madrid. Un
boschetto chiuso. Notte chiara.*

**DON CARLO**

(*Leggendo un biglietto*)

"A mezzanotte, ai giardin della Regina,
Sotto gli allôr della fonte vicina."
È mezzanotte; mi par udire
Il mormorio del vicino fonte . . .
Ebbro d'amor, ebbro di gioia il core!
Elisabetta! mio ben! mio tesor! a me
vien!

(*Entra Eboli velata.*)

**DON CARLO**

(*Sottovoce ad Eboli da lui creduta la
Regina*)

Sei tu, sei tu, bell'adorata,
Che appari in mezzo ai fior!
Sei tu, l'alma beata
Già scorda il suo dolor!
O tu cagion del mio contento,
Parlarti posso almen!
O tu cagion del mio tormento,
Sei tu, amor mio, sei tu, mio ben!

**PHILIP**

Dreamer so strange and young!
You could not speak like this,
If you would know the heart of man
As Philip has known it.
But no more!
The King has heard nothing!
Have no fear!
But beware of the Grand Inquisitor!

**RODRIGO**

Why . . . ! ? Sire!

**PHILIP**

You have remained in my royal pres-
ence,
And yet you have not asked
A favor of the King.
I want to keep you near me from now
on!

**RODRIGO**

Sire, no! I should prefer
To be what I am now!

**PHILIP**

You are too proud!
Although your searching eyes have seen
The trials of my kingdom,
You cannot know the bitter sorrow
Rending my heart and disturbing my
soul.
Cold and dark is my palace,
And haunted by misfortune . . .
A wife whom I adore . . .
Yet whom I trust no more!

**RODRIGO**

Sire, what are you saying?

**PHILIP**

The Queen . . . I am racked by suspicion . . .
Don Carlo . . .

RODRIGO (*quickly*)

His heart is pure and noble!

PHILIP (*breaking out in pain*)

What could ever replace
What Carlo stole from me?

(*Rodrigo looks at the King in wordless
apprehension.*)

I shall entrust their fate to you.
Read in their hearts
Now rent with heedless passion!
You shall always be free
To encounter the Queen.
Vainly searching for one
Since his reign began,
In you at last
The King has found a man!

**RODRIGO**

(*aside, overwhelmed with joy*)

(Out of the night a star so bright and
fair
Has filled with light
His heart so full of dark despair!)

**PHILIP**

You alone! Ah could I know once more
The peace I knew before!

**RODRIGO**

(Of hope and light to dream!
Oh ray of hope and glory!)

PHILIP (*darkly*)

Beware of the Grand Inquisitor!
Be careful! Be careful!

**RODRIGO**

Sire!

(*The King extends his hand to Rodrigo
who kisses it while kneeling down.*)

(*The curtain falls quickly.*)


## ACT THREE

### SCENE 1

*The Queen's Gardens in Madrid. A
secluded grove with a fountain. It is
a clear night.*

**DON CARLO**

(*reading a note*)

"At midnight, in the Gardens of the
Queen, near the arbor by the little
fountain."
Midnight has sounded. I seem to hear
The gentle murmur of the little foun-
tain.
Tremble, my heart, raving,
Insane with passion! Elizabeth,
My love, my delight! Ah, come!

(*Eboli enters, her face hidden by a
veil. Don Carlo believes her to be
the Queen and addresses her passionately.*)

'Tis you, yes, you, my love so tender
Who stands before my eyes!
'Tis true, 'tis you! Your radiant
splendor
Defies this cruel disguise.
Oh, you who hold my heart undying,
At last you heard my plea!
Oh, you who coldly spurned my crying,
Will now return your heart to me!

EBOLI (*Tra sè*)

Un tanto amor è gioia a me suprema.
Amata, amata io son!

DON CARLO

L'universo obbliam! te sola, o cara, io
  bramo!
Passato più non ho, non penso all'-
  avvenir!
Io t'amo, io t'amo!

EBOLI

Possa l'amor . . . il tuo cor . . . al mio
  cor, . . .
Il tuo cor . . . sempre unir!

DON CARLO

L'universo obbliam, la vita e il ciel
  istesso!
Io t'amo, io t'amo!

EBOLI

Oh! gioia suprema!

(*Togliendosi la maschera*)

DON CARLO (*Atterrito, tra sè*)

(Ciel! Non è la Regina!)

EBOLI

Ahimè! Qual mai pensiero vi tien
  pallido,
Immoto, e fa gelido il labbro?
Quale spettro si leva fra noi?
Non credete al mio cor,
Che sol batte per voi?

(*Con passione*)

V'è ignoto forse, ignoto ancora
Qual fier agguato a' piedi vostri sta?
Sul vostro capo ad ora la folgore del
  ciel piombar potrà!

DON CARLO

Deh! nol credete: ad ora più denso
vedo delle nubi il vel;
Su questo capo io veggo ognora
Pronta a scoppiar la folgore del ciel!

EBOLI

Udii dal padre, da Posa istesso
In tuon sinistro di voi parlar.

DON CARLO

Rodrigo!

EBOLI

Salvarvi poss'io. Io v'amo.

DON CARLO

Qual mistero a me si rivelò!

EBOLI (*Inquieta*)

Ah! Carlo!

DON CARLO

Il vostro inver celeste è un core,
Ma chiuso il mio restar al gaudio dè!
Noi facemmo ambedue un sogno strano
In notte si gentil, tra il profumo dei
  fior.

EBOLI

Un sogno! O ciel! Quelle parole
  ardenti
Ad altra credeste rivolgere illuso!
Qual balen! qual mister!
Voi la regina amate!

DON CARLO (*Atterrito*)

Pietà!

RODRIGO

Che disse mai? Egli è deliro, non merta
  fè . . .
Demente egli è!

EBOLI

Io nel suo cor lessi l'amor; or noto è a
  me . . .
Ei si perdè.

RODRIGO

(*Con accento terribile*)

Che vuol dir?

EBOLI

Tutto io so!

RODRIGO

Che vuol dir? Sciagurata!
Trema! io son . . .

EBOLI

L'intimo sei . . . del Re . . . Ignoto
  non è a me.
Ma una nemica io son formidabil,
  possente:
M'è noto il tuo poter, il mio t'e ignoto
  ancor!

RODRIGO

Che mai pretendi dir?

EBOLI

Nulla!
(*Cupo ed a mezza voce a Rodrigo*)
Al mio furor·sfuggite invano,
Il suo destin è in questa mano.

EBOLI (*aside*)

Enchanted moment of profound emotion!
Carlo loves me. His heart is mine!

DON CARLO

So forever farewell,
Farewell to tears and sorrow!
Forgotten the world,
Forgotten pain and strife!
I love you! I love you!

EBOLI

Now that you found me,
May your passion surround me
To the end of my life!

DON CARLO

Like the stars in the sky
My love shall last forever!
I love you forever!

EBOLI

I love you forever!

(*She removes her veil.*)

DON CARLO

(*aghast, to himself*)

(God! It is not the Queen!)

EBOLI

Oh Carlo! What sudden notion
Has disturbed your mind?
You tremble, and your brow
Has turned pale . . .
Is it fear that I may not be true?
Are you doubting my heart,
Which beats only for you?

(*Carlo does not answer.*)

You cannot know what all around you
The evil forces of the Court have
planned.
Beloved, ever since I found you
I fear for you, I fear their deadly hand.

DON CARLO

I know the dangers that surround me,
The traitors who have made
The prince their game,
And all the forces that confound me
May soon combine to end my life in
shame.

EBOLI

I heard your father and your friend
Posa
In hateful words discuss
Don Carlo's heart.

DON CARLO

Rodrigo!

EBOLI

The one who can save you,
See her in me, for I love you!

DON CARLO

What she tells me
Turns my heart to stone.

EBOLI (*worried*)

Ah, Carlo!

DON CARLO

Your loving heart is great and noble,
But mine cannot take part
In joyful play.
We were both in a dream,
In a dream of enchantment
Wrought by the beautiful night
And the spell of the moon.

EBOLI

Don Carlo! A dream . . . those words
Of love and passion were meant for
  another . . . 'twas all a mistake!
Now I see! Yes, I see:
You love the Queen!

DON CARLO (*losing control*)

'Tis true!

RODRIGO (*entering rapidly*)

What did he say? He must be raving.
Yes, it is plain: He is insane.

EBOLI

There is no doubt: I have found out
What to your friend will mean the end!

RODRIGO

(*in a menacing tone*)

What do you mean?

EBOLI

Now I know!

RODRIGO

What do you mean, vicious viper?
Tremble! I am . . .

EBOLI

You are the King's companion.
You see, I know you well.
I have no fear of you,
For I, too, can be dangerous.
Your power I can assess,
But you do not know mine.

RODRIGO

What do you mean by this?

EBOLI

Nothing!

(*with subdued but unmistakable meaning, to Rodrigo*)

My woman's heart you have offended.
Only revenge will ever mend it.

RODRIGO (*Ad Eboli*)
Parlar dovete, a noi svelate
Qual mai pensiero vi trasse qui.

EBOLI

Io son la tigre al cor, al cor ferita,
Alla vendetta l'offesa invita.

RODRIGO

Su voi del ciel cadrà il furor.
Degli innocenti è il protettor.

DON CARLO

Stolto fui! Oh destin spietato!
D'una madre ho il nome macchiato!
Sol Iddio indagar potrà
Se questo cor colpa non ha.

EBOLI

Ah! voi m'avete in cor ferita,
Alla vendetta l'offesa invita,
Il mio furore sfuggite invano,
È il destin in questa mano.

RODRIGO

Parlar dovete, a noi svelate
Qual mai pensier vi trasse qui.

EBOLI (*Con ironia amara*)
Ed io . . . che tremava al suo cospetto!
Ella volea, questa santa novella,
Di celesti virtù mascherando il suo cor,
Il piacere libar ed intera la coppa
    vuotar dell'amor.
Ah per mia fè! fu ben ardita!

RODRIGO

(*Snudando il pugnale*)
Tu qui morrai.

DON CARLO (*Trattenendolo*)
Rodrigo!

RODRIGO

Il velen ancora non stillò quel labbro
    maledetto!

DON CARLO

Rodrigo, frena il cor!

EBOLI

Perchè tardi a ferir?

RODRIGO

No.

EBOLI

Non indugiar ancor!

RODRIGO

No.

EBOLI

Perchè tardi?

RODRIGO

(*Gettando il pugnale*)
No, una speme mi resta;
M'ispirerà il Signor.

EBOLI

Trema per te, falso figliuolo,
La mia vendetta arriva già.
Trema per te, fra poco il suolo
Sotto il tuo piè si schiuderà!

DON CARLO

Tutt'ella sa! tremendo duolo!
Oppresso il cor, forza non ha.
Tutto ella sa! nè ancora il suolo
Sotto il mio piè si schiuderà!

RODRIGO

Tacer tu dêi: rispetta il duolo,
O un Dio sever ti punirà.
Tacer tu dêi, o per te il suolo
Sotto il tuo piè si schiuderà!

(*Eboli esce furibonda*)
Carlo! se mai su te fogli importanti
    serbi,
Qualche nota, un segreto, a me affi-
    darli dêi.

DON CARLO (*Esitando*)
A te! all'intimo del Re!

RODRIGO

Sospetti tu di me?

DON CARLO

No, no, del mio cor sei la speranza:
Questo cor che sì t'amò
A te chiudere non so.
In te riposi ogni fidanza:
Sì, questi fogli importanti ti do!

RODRIGO

Carlo, tu puoi fidare in me.

DON CARLO

Io m'abbandono a te.
(*Si gettano nelle braccia l'un all'altro.*)

**RODRIGO** (*to Eboli*)
I want to know what brought you here,
What evil mischance
Has made you appear.

**EBOLI**
Just like a tigress, wild and bleeding,
I'll tear my foes before receding.

**RODRIGO**
Let God the course of justice chart!
Heaven alone can read our heart.

**DON CARLO**
Through my folly, my folly,
My raving madness
I have turned my delight into sadness!
Only He who guides the stars on high,
He can save our souls. Ah let me die!

**EBOLI**
My woman's heart you have offended.
Only revenge will ever mend it.
Because you scorn my deepest passion
You'll try in vain to flee my wrath.

**RODRIGO**
I want to know what brought you here,
What evil demon made you appear.

**EBOLI** (*with bitter irony*)
And I, I who trembled before her!
She who so chaste, so demure
And so saintly, like an angel so pure
From the heavenly choir,
Found the time to be gay
And to drink to the dregs
From the cup of desire!
Ah, by my faith! A splendid actress!

**RODRIGO**
(*drawing his dagger*)
You have to die.

**DON CARLO**
(*restraining him*)
Rodrigo!

**RODRIGO**
Like the snake that must be killed
Before spilling its poison!

**DON CARLO** (*to Rodrigo*)
Rodrigo! Not that!

**EBOLI**
What is staying your hand?

**RODRIGO**
No.

**EBOLI**
Kill me and make an end!

**RODRIGO**
No.

**EBOLI**
What prevents you?

**RODRIGO**
(*throwing the dagger away*)
One single hope I have left now.
The Lord will give me strength.

**EBOLI** (*to Don Carlo*)
Dread and dismay shall strike with
   horror
Into your heart their blinding flash!
When my revenge I'll have tomorrow,
Vile and corrupt, your world will crash.

**DON CARLO**
It is too late! Desperate sorrow!
My heart is lost, my will is gone!
It is too late, for by tomorrow
Crumbling to dust, my world will crash.

**RODRIGO**
Do not betray his bitter sorrow,
Or you shall rue your deed too rash!
Do not betray him, or tomorrow
Over your head the world will crash!

(*Eboli exits in wild fury*)

Carlo, if you have on you certain notes
   and papers of importance, maybe
   secret . . .
Entrust them to my care!

**DON CARLO** (*hesitating*)
To you, the King's most trusted friend?

**RODRIGO**
Have you lost faith in me?

**DON CARLO**
No, no! You alone in all Creation,
You alone can know the woe
Of this heart that loved you so.
My friend, my only way to salvation!
Here, take my letters and papers in
   trust!

**RODRIGO**
Carlo, I vow my life to you!

**DON CARLO**
I hand my life to you.

(*They fall into each other's arms.*)

## SCENA 2

*Una gran piazza innanzi Nostra Donna d'Atocha. A destra la Chiesa, cui conduce una grande scala. A sinistra un palazzo. In fondo altra scalinata che scende ad una piazza inferiore in mezzo alla quale si eleva un rogo di cui si vede la cima.*

*(Le campane suonano a festa. La calca, contenuta appena dagli Alabardieri, invade la scena.)*

CORO DI POPOLO

Spuntato ecco il dì d'esultanza,
Onore al più grande dei Regi!
In esso hanno i popol fidanza,
Il mondo è prostrato al suo piè!
Il nostro amor ovunque l'accompagna,
E questo amor giammai, non scemerà.
Il nome suo è l'orgoglio della Spagna,
E viver deve nell'eternità . . .

*(Si ode una marcia funebre.)*

CORO DI FRATI

*(Che traversa la scena, conducendo i condannati del Santo Uffizio)*

Il dì spuntò, dì del terrore,
Il dì tremendo, il dì feral.
Morran, morran! giusto è il rigore,
Dell'Immortal!
Ma di perdón voce suprema
All'anatema succederà,
Se il peccator all'ora estrema
Si pentirà!

*(Rodrigo, il Conte di Lerma, Elisabetta, Tebaldo, Paggi, Dame, Signori della Corte, Araldi Reali.)*

*(Marcia. Il corteggio esce dal palagio. Tutte le corporazioni dello Stato, tutta la Corte, i Deputati di tutte le provincie dell'Impero. I Grandi di Spagna. Rodrigo è in mezzo ad essi. La Regina in mezzo alle Dame. Tebaldo porta il manto d'Elisabetta. Paggi, ecc. Il corteggio si schiera innanzi ai gradini della Chiesa.)*

CORO DI POPOLO

Onor al Re! Ei vivrà nell'eternità!

L'ARALDO REALE E IL POPOLO

*(Innanzi alla Chiesa la cui porta è ancora chiusa, tutti si scoprono il capo)*

Schiusa or sia la porta del tempio!
O magion del Signor, t'apri omai!
Sacrario venerato, a noi rendi il nostro Re!

*(Le porte della Chiesa nell'aprirsi lascian vedere Filippo con la corona sul capo, incedendo sotto un baldacchino in mezzo ai frati. I Signori s'inchinano, il popolo si prostra. I Grandi si coprono il capo.)*

FILIPPO

Nel posar sul mio capo la corona,
Popol', giurai al ciel,
Che me la dona,
Dar morte ai rei col fuoco e con l'acciar.

CORO DI POPOLO

Gloria a Filippo! Gloria al ciel!
*(Tutti s'inchinano silenziosi. Filippo scende i gradini del tempio e va a prendere la mano d'Elisabetta per continuare il suo cammino. I sei Deputati Fiamminghi, vestiti a bruno, si presentano all'improvviso, condotti da Don Carlo, e si gettano ai piedi di Filippo.)*

ELISABETTA *(Tra sè)*

(Qui Carlo! O ciel!)

RODRIGO *(Tra sè)*

(Qual pensier lo sospinge!)

FILIPPO

Chi son costor prostrati innanzi a me?

DON CARLO

Son messaggier' del Brabante
E di Fiandra ch'il tuo figliuol
Adduce innanzi al Re.

DEPUTATI

Sire, Sire, no, l'ora estrema
Ancora non suonò per i Fiamminghi in duol.
Tutt'un popolo t'implora,
Fa che in pianto così sempre non gema.

SCENE 2

*A vast square in front of the Cathedral of Our Lady of Atocha. To the right, the church, with an impressive flight of steps leading up to it. To the left, a palace. To the rear, another flight of steps seems to lead to a lower square in the center of which a stake has been erected whose top can be seen. The horizon is formed by large buildings and distant hills.*

*(The sound of festive bells is heard. A milling crowd, held in check with difficulty by halberdiers, fills the stage.)*

CHORUS OF THE PEOPLE

Rejoicing today in this royal display,
We honor King Philip in grateful prostration.
We pledge him our faith, and that loyal we stay,
As his name shall resound and his fame be renowned
To the end of Creation!

*(A funeral march is heard. A group of monks is crossing the stage, leading those condemned by the Inquisition towards the stake.)*

CHORUS OF MONKS

The day has come, the day of terror,
The day of judgment, the day of death.
To die, to die behooves the sinner.
Just and great is the will of the Immortal.
But in the end a voice from Heaven
Will lift the ban from the soul of those
Who will renounce in true repentance
Their evil thoughts of sin and revolt.

*(The populace, having remained silent for a moment, resume their joyous tribute as the monks disappear and the bells start sounding again.)*

*(Rodrigo, the Count of Lerma, Elizabeth, Theobald, pages, ladies-in-waiting, gentlemen of the realm, and heralds now enter in a solemn procession from the palace. All the state offices, the court, the imperial deputies from the Spanish provinces, are represented. The procession comes to a halt in front of the church steps.)*

CHORUS OF THE PEOPLE

Long live the King! Glory to his reign!
*(A Herald, seconded by the people, addresses himself to the portals of the church which are still closed. Everyone bares his head.)*

Open wide, you portals of mercy,
Open wide, holy house of the Lord!
Oh sacred Shrine of Faith,
Give to his people their King!

*(When the church portals open, we see King Philip in full regalia, the golden crown on his head, standing under a canopy, surrounded by monks. The grandees bow, while the people kneel down. The nobles cover their heads.)*

PHILIP

When I first placed the crown upon my head, my people,
I swore to God whose grace had crowned me,
To root out evil
By fire and by sword.

CHORUS OF THE PEOPLE

Praise be King Philip!
Praise be God!

*(Everyone bows in silence. Philip descends the stairs and takes the Queen's hand in order to continue the procession. All at once, six Flemish deputies, clad in brown, appear, led by Don Carlo. They kneel at the King's feet.)*

ELIZABETH *(aside)*

(Don Carlo! 'Tis he!)

RODRIGO *(aside)*

(What has moved him to come here?)

PHILIP

Who are these men
Before me on their knees?

DON CARLO

They have been sent
From Brabant and Flanders,
And your own son has brought them
To see the King.

THE DEPUTIES

Sire, Sire!
Sorrow and grief have brought us here, my Lord,
To speak for Flanders.
Steeped in tears, the
Flemish people look to you in their plea
For rightful mercy.

Se pietoso il tuo core la clemenza
E la pace chiedea nel tempio,
Pietà di noi ti prenda, di noi pietà,
E salva il nostro suolo,
O Re, che avesti il tuo poter da Dio.

### FILIPPO

A Dio voi foste infidi,
Infidi al vostro Re.
Son i Fiamminghi a me ribelli:
Guardie, guardie, vadan lontan da me.

### ELISABETTA, TEBALDO, DON CARLO, RODRIGO E CORO DI POPOLO

Su di lor stenda il Re la sua mano
    sovrana,
Trovi pietà, signor, il Fiammingo nel
    duol,
Nel suo martir presso a morir
Ahi! manda già l'estremo sospir.

### SEI FRATI

Ah! son costor infidi,
In Dio non han la fè,
Vedete in lor sol dei ribelli,
Tutto il rigor mertan del Re.
Salva il nostro suol, o Re!

### DON CARLO

Sir! egli è tempo ch'io viva.
Stanco son di seguir una esistenza
    oscura,
In questo suol!
Se Dio vuol che il tuo serto
Questa mia fronte un giorno a cinger
    venga,
Per la Spagna prepara un Re degno di
    lei!
Il Brabante e la Fiandra a me tu dona.

### FILIPPO

Insensato! chieder tanto ardisci!
Tu vuoi ch'io stesso porga a te
L'acciar che un dì immolerebbe il Re!

### DON CARLO

Ah! Dio legge a noi nei cor;
Ei giudicar ci dè.

### ELISABETTA

Io tremo!

### RODRIGO

Ei si perdè!

### DON CARLO (*Snudando la spada*)

Io qui lo giuro al ciel!
Sarò tuo salvator,
Popol fiammingo, io sol!

### TUTTI E CORO

L'acciar! innanzi al Re!
L'infante è fuor di sè.

### FILIPPO

Guardie! disarmato ei sia!
Signor, sostegni del mio trono,
Disarmato ei sia.
Ma che? nessuno?

### DON CARLO

Or ben, di voi chi l'oserà?
A quest'acciar chi sfuggirà?
(*I Grandi di Spagna indietreggiano innanzi a Don Carlo. Il Re furente afferra la spada del Comandante delle Guardie, che gli sta presso.*)

### FILIPPO

Disarmato ei sia!

### RODRIGO (*A Don Carlo*)

A me il ferro.

### DON CARLO

O ciel! Tu! Rodrigo!
(*Don Carlo rimette la sua spada a Rodrigo, che s'inchina nel presentarla al Re.*)

### CORO
Egli! Posa!

### ELISABETTA
Ei!

### FILIPPO

Marchese, Duca siete.
Andiam . . . or alla festa.
(*Il Re s'incammina dando la mano alla Regina; la Corte lo segue. Vanno a prender posto nella tribuna a loro riservata per l'auto-da-fè.*)

### CORO DI POPOLO

Spuntato è il dì
D'esultanza, onor al Re!
In esso hanno i popol fidanza,
Il mondo è prostrato al suo piè!

### SEI FRATI

Il dì spuntò del terrore!

### UNA VOCE DAL CIELO
(*Molto lontana*)

Volate, verso il ciel,
Volate, povere alme,
V'affrettate a goder
La pace del Signore!

Heaven's glory has crowned you:
Let its mercy surround you
And fill your heart with peace!
Oh Sire, grant us your pity in our distress,
Show us compassion,
And spare our beloved land!
Oh, spare the soil of Flanders,
King, whom God himself lent might
and honor!

PHILIP

The God whom you've offended?
The King whom you betray?
You Flemish traitors, go from me!
Guards, take these insurgents away!

ELIZABETH, TEBALDO, DON CARLO,
RODRIGO, AND CHORUS OF THE PEOPLE
May the King in his heart
Grant them grace and compassion!
May they find mercy, Lord,
In their bitter despair!
Oh Lord, no more of strife and war!
Ah, hear them cry! They must not die.
Let Flanders find relief!

SIX MONKS

The Lord they have offended,
The holy faith they have betrayed.
Their evil heart upholds rebellion.
Their bold uprising must be crushed.

DON CARLO

Sire! I shall hide it no longer:
I am weary of leading
An existence of leisure
Here at your court.
If one day, by the will of God,
Your mantle shall fall
On my shoulders,
It is time you prepare me
For crown and royal duty.
To command over Flanders
You shall name me!

PHILIP

It is madness to request such a favor!
You wish that I should hand you
The sword which you, one day,
Will turn against the King.

DON CARLO

Ah! God can read my heart.
He alone will judge us all.

ELIZABETH

I tremble!

RODRIGO

He went too far!

DON CARLO
(drawing his sword)
So help me God! I swear:
It is I, I alone,
Through whom Flanders shall live!

ALL EXCEPT PHILIP AND CARLO
The sword before the King!
The Prince has lost his mind.

PHILIP

Guards! Go ahead and disarm him!
My lords, gentlemen of the realm,
He must be disarmed.
There's no one? There's no one?

DON CARLO

I dare you come and take my sword.
You stay away or will be gored!
(The grandees retreat before Don
Carlo. Furiously, the King seizes the
sword of the Commander of the
Guard who stands next to him.)

PHILIP
Go ahead! Disarm him!

RODRIGO (to Don Carlo)
Hand me your weapon!

DON CARLO
Oh God! You . . . Rodrigo?
(Don Carlo hands the sword to Rod-
rigo who bows and presents it to the
King.)
CHORUS
He? . . . Posa!

ELIZABETH
He!
PHILIP
Marquis, from now on duke!
And now let us proceed!
(The King, taking the Queen's hand,
resumes the procession. Their en-
tourage follows them to their seats
where they are to watch the Auto-
da-Fé.)

CHORUS OF THE PEOPLE
May long live the King!
His praises we sing
In grateful prostration.
We pledge him today that loyal we stay
To the end of Creation.

SIX MONKS
The day has come, the day of terror!

A VOICE FROM HEAVEN
(from far off)
Arise and come to me,
Where at last you will be free
And shall find rest
And peace in Heaven.

SEI DEPUTATI

(*Sul davanti della scena, mentre il rogo s'accende*)

E puoi soffrirlo, o ciel!
Nè spegni quelle fiamme!
S'accende in nome tuo quel rogo
   punitor!

SEI FRATI

Il dì tremendo, il dì feral!

SEI DEPUTATI

E in nome del Signor
L'accende l'oppressor!

FILIPPO, SEI FRATI E CORO

Gloria al ciel!

SEI DEPUTATI

E tu lo soffri, o ciel!

(*La fiamma s'alza dal rogo.*)


ATTO QUARTO

SCENA 1

*Il Gabinetto del Re a Madrid. Il Re assorto in profonda meditazione, appoggiato ad un tavolo ingombro di carte, ove due doppieri finiscono di consumarsi. L'alba rischiara già le invetriate delle finestre.*

FILIPPO (*Come trasognato*)

Ella giammai m'amò!
No! quel cor chiuso è a me,
Amor per me non ha!
Io la rivedo ancor
Contemplar triste in volto
Il mio crin bianco il dì
Che qui di Francia venne.
No, amor per me non ha!

(*Ritornando in sè*)

Ove son? Quei doppier presso a finir!
L'aurora imbianca il mio veron . . .
Già spunta il dì.
Passar veggo i miei giorni lenti!
Il sonno, o Dio, sparì da' miei occhi
   languenti.
Dormirò sol nel manto mio regal,

Quando la mia giornata è giunta a
   sera,
Dormirò sol sotto la vôlta nera,
Là nell'avello dell'Escurial.
Se il serto regal a me desse il poter
Di leggere nei cor,
Che Dio può sol veder!
Se dorme il prence, veglia il traditore!
Il serto perde il re, il consorte l'onore!
Dormirò sol nel manto mio regal,
Quando la mia giornata è giunta a
   sera,
Dormirò sol sotto la vôlta nera
Là nell'avello dell'Escurial.
Ah! se il serto regal
A me desse il poter di leggere nei cor!
Ella giammai mi amò! No! Quel cor
   chiuso m'è,
Amor per me non ha, amor per me
   non ha!

(*Ricade nelle sue meditazioni.*)

IL CONTE DI LERMA

Il Grand'Inquisitor!

(*Il Grande Inquisitore, vegliardo di novant'anni e cieco, entra sostenuto da due frati domenicani.*)

INQUISITORE

Son io dinanzi al Re?

FILIPPO

Sì, vi feci chiamar, mio padre!
In dubbio io son.
Carlo mi colma il cor
D'una tristezza amara;
L'Infante è a me ribelle,
Armossi contro il padre.

INQUISITORE

Qual mezzo per punir scegli tu?

FILIPPO

Mezzo estrem.

INQUISITORE

Noto mi sia!

FILIPPO

Che fugga . . . o che la scure . . .

INQUISITORE

Ebben?

FILIPPO

Se il filio a morte invio,
M'assolve la tua mano?

SIX DEPUTIES

(*watching from downstage as the stake starts burning*)

And Heaven can look on!
The flames remain ignited.
They desecrate His name
By fire and by sword.

SIX MONKS

The day of terror, the day of Death!
The day of judgment and of Death!

SIX DEPUTIES

By fire and by sword
They desecrate the Lord!

PHILIP, SIX MONKS, AND CHORUS

Glory be!

SIX DEPUTIES

And Heaven can look on!

(*The stake goes up in flames.*)
(*Curtain.*)


## ACT FOUR

### SCENE 1

*The King's study in Madrid.*

(*Philip II, deep in thought, sitting at a table strewn with papers. Two candles are nearly burnt down. Dawn starts breaking, lighting the window.*)

PHILIP

(*as if in a dream*)

I never won her heart!
No! It never was mine,
Her heart was never mine,
Was never mine!
I still can see her eyes
Looking, sad and bewildered,
At my grey hair, when first
She came from France to meet me.
No, her heart was never mine,
Her heart was never mine!

(*coming awake*)

Where am I?
The candles are about to die
Before the slowly rising dawn.
The day is here!
A day, grey and endlessly creeping!
Burning, my eyes can no more
Find respite in sleeping.
Lonely and cold,
Laid out in shrouds of gold,
I shall find peace,
My journey will be ended.
Night will enfold

The one whose soul ascended
Onward to God, the Lord in Heaven,
Out of the silent tomb at Escurial.
Why cannot the crown
Lend my searching eyes the power
To read the human heart's
Innermost thoughts, dark and secret?
While the King slumbers,
Silently lurks the traitor,
To steal from him his crown,
And his wife, and his honor.
Lonely and cold,
Laid out in shrouds of gold,
I shall find peace,
My journey will be ended.
Night will enfold
The one whose soul ascended
Onward to God, the Lord in Heaven,
Out of the silent tomb at Escurial.
Ah! Why cannot the crown
Lend my senses the power
To read the human heart? ! . . .
I never won her heart!
No, it never was mine!
Her heart was never mine!

(*He again loses himself in his thoughts.*)

THE COUNT OF LERMA

The Grand Inquisitor!

(*The Grand Inquisitor, ninety years old and blind, enters. He is supported by two Dominican friars.*)

GRAND INQUISITOR

Am I before the King?

PHILIP

Yes. I bade you come here, my father.
I am in doubt.
Carlo has plunged my heart
Into despair and sadness.
He even drew his sword
Against his royal father.

GRAND INQUISITOR

What punishment can fit such a crime?

PHILIP

Only one!

GRAND INQUISITOR

But in what way?

PHILIP

While fleeing . . . by execution . . .

GRAND INQUISITOR

Well then?

PHILIP

If I permit his death,
Can I obtain your pardon?

INQUISITORE

La pace dell'impero i dì val d'un
ribelle.

FILIPPO

Posso il figlio immolar al mondo, io
cristian?

INQUISITORE

Per riscattarci Iddio . . . il suo sacrificò.

FILIPPO

Ma tu puoi dar vigor a legge sì severa?

INQUISITORE

Ovunque avrà vigor, se sul Calvario
l'ebbe.

FILIPPO

La natura, l'amor tacer potranno in
me?

INQUISITORE

Tutto tacer dovrà per esaltar la fé.

FILIPPO

Sta ben!

INQUISITORE

Non vuol il Re su d'altro interrogarmi?

FILIPPO

No.

INQUISITORE

Allor son io ch'a voi parlerò, Sire.
Nell'ispano suol mai l'eresia dominò,
Ma v'ha chi vuol minar l'edifizio divin.
L'amico egli è del Re, il suo fedel
compagno,
Il dèmon tentator che lo spinge a
rovina.
Di Carlo il tradimento, che giunse a
t'irritar,
In paragon del suo futile gioco appar.
Ed io . . . l'Inquisitor, io che levai
sovente
Sopra orde vil' di rei la mano mia
possente,
Pei grandi di quaggiù, scordando la
mia fè,
Tranquilli lascio andar . . . un gran
ribelle . . .
E il Re.

FILIPPO

Per traversar i dì dolenti in cui viviamo
Nella mia Corte invan cercat'ho quel
che bramo.
Un uomo! Un cuor leal . . . Io lo
trovai!

INQUISITORE

Perchè un uomo?
Perchè allor il nome hai tu di Re,
Sire, s'alcun v'ha pari a te?

FILIPPO

Non più, frate!

INQUISITORE

Le idee dei novator in te son penetrate!
Infrangere tu vuoi con la tua debol
man
Il santo giogo esteso sovra l'orbe
roman!
Ritorna al tuo dover; la Chiesa all'uom
che spera,
A chi si pente, puote offrir la venia
intera:
A te chiedo il Signor di Posa.

FILIPPO

No, giammai!

INQUISITORE

O Re, se non foss'io con te nel regio
ostel
Oggi stesso, lo giuro a Dio, doman
saresti
Presso il Grande Inquisitor al tribunal
supremo.

FILIPPO

Frate! troppo soffrii il tuo parlar
crudel!

INQUISITORE

Perchè evocar allor l'ombra di Samuel?
Dato ho finor due Regi al regno tuo
possente!
L'opra di tanti dì tu vuoi strugger,
demente!
Perchè mi trovo io qui? Che vuol il
Re da me?

(*Per uscire*)

FILIPPO

Mio padre, che tra noi la pace alberghi
ancor.

INQUISITORE

La pace?

(*Allontanandosi sempre*)

GRAND INQUISITOR

The safety of the kingdom
Does not allow rebellion.

PHILIP

How can I, a Christian father,
Kill my son?

GRAND INQUISITOR

God, in order to redeem us,
Has sacrificed His own.

PHILIP

But how can you sustain
A law so harsh and fearful?

GRAND INQUISITOR

What Calvary sustains
Does not demand my sanction.

PHILIP

Will not love and regret
Forever haunt my days?

GRAND INQUISITOR

In service to the Faith
We win the highest praise.

PHILIP

So be it!

GRAND INQUISITOR

Have you, oh King,
No more you wish to ask me?

PHILIP

No.

GRAND INQUISITOR

Then it is I who must speak to you,
  Sire!
Never here in Spain has heresy won
  ground,
Despite the cunning schemes
Of the foes of our Faith.
But now the King himself
Has chosen as companion
A most dangerous fiend
Bent on nothing but treason.
Don Carlo's own rebellion,
Which comes to bitter end,
Seems innocent and childish
Against that of your friend.
And I remain alone,
Heaven's devout defender,
More mighty than the throne
And all its pomp and splendor.
Here I stand idly by,
While loud with treason ring
The voices of the traitor
And of his patron, the King!

PHILIP

In times like these the King himself
Needs someone near him,
Other than those at court,
Who fawn because they fear him, . . .
A man, a trusted friend,
And I have found one.

GRAND INQUISITOR

You need a friend?
Why then grandly call yourself a king,
Sire, if you feel the need for equals?

PHILIP

Enough, Priest!

GRAND INQUISITOR

Already I perceive
The canker of subversion!
The spirit of dissent
Now rules the royal home,
To break the gentle yoke
That ties the world to Rome!
Your duty now is clear.
The Church can ease the sentence
Of sinners who confess
And pine in true repentance.
I demand that you hand me Posa!

PHILIP

No, not that!

GRAND INQUISITOR

Oh King, had you not called me here
To hear your secret confession,
I swear to God, you would appear
Before the Sacred Court
And find a jury without mercy.

PHILIP

Silence! How dare you, priest,
To talk to me like that?

GRAND INQUISITOR

Why then conjure again
Shadows of Samuel?
Two Kings owe me their power;
In peace they could enjoy it.
What in devotion I wrought,
Must your folly destroy it?!
But why am I still here?
What is the King's command?
(He is about to leave.)

PHILIP

My Father, let between us
Agreement be restored!

GRAND INQUISITOR

Agreement?
(He proceeds on his way out.)

FILIPPO
Obbliar tu dêi quel ch'è passato.

INQUISITORE
(Sulla porta per uscire)
Forse!

FILIPPO
Dunque il trono piegar dovrà sempre
all'altare!

ELISABETTA
(Entra, e si getta ai piedi del Re)
Giustizia, giustizia, Sire!
Ho fè nella lealtà del Re.
Son nella Corte tua crudelmente trat-
tata
E da nemici oscuri, incogniti
oltraggiata.
Lo scrigno ov'io chiudea, Sire, tutt'un
tesor,
I gioielli . . . altri oggetti a me più
cari ancor . . .
L'hanno rapito a me! Giustizia! la
reclamo da Vostra Maestà.

(Il Re si alza lentamente, prende un
cofanetto dal tavolo e lo presenta
alla Regina.)

FILIPPO
Quello che voi cercate, eccolo!

ELISABETTA
Ciel!

FILIPPO
A voi d'aprirlo piaccia.
(La Regina rifuta d'un cenno.)
Ebben, io l'aprirò!
(Infrangendo il cofanetto)

ELISABETTA (Tra sè)
(Ah! mi sento morir!)

FILIPPO
Il ritratto di Carlo!
Non trovate parola?

ELISABETTA
Sì.

FILIPPO
Fra i vostri gioiel'?

ELISABETTA
Sì!

FILIPPO
Che! confessar l'osate a me?

ELISABETTA
Io l'oso! sì!
Ben lo sapete, un dì promessa
Al figlio vostro fu la mia man!
Or v'appartengo a Dio sommessa,
Ma immacolata qual giglio son!
Ed ora si sospetta l'onor d'Elisabetta!
Si dubita di me . . . e chi m'oltraggia è
il Re!

FILIPPO
Ardita troppo voi favellate!
Me debole credete e sfidarmi sembrate;
La debolezza in me può diventar furor.
Tremate allor per voi, per me!

ELISABETTA
Il mio fallir qual'è?

FILIPPO
Spergiura! se tanta infamia colmò,
La misura,
Se fui da voi, se fui tradito,
Io lo giuro, lo giuro innanzi al ciel,
Il sangue verserò!

ELISABETTA
Pietà mi fate . . .

FILIPPO
Ah! la pietà d'adultera consorte!

ELISABETTA (Cade svenuta)
Ah!

FILIPPO
(Aprendo le porte dal fondo)
Soccorso alla Regina!

EBOLI
(Spaventata al veder la Regina sven-
uta)
(Ciel! che mai feci! Ahimè!)

RODRIGO (A Filippo)
Sire! Soggetta è a voi la metà della
terra.
Sareste dunque in tanto vasto imper
il sol . . .
Cui non v'è dato il comandar?

PHILIP

You must forget all that was spoken.

GRAND INQUISITOR
(*in the doorway*)

Must I?

PHILIP

Should the throne capitulate again
Before the altar?!

(*The Queen enters, very excited, and
throws herself at the King's feet.*)

ELIZABETH

Oh help me, oh help me, Sire!
For justice I plead . . .
The King will not deny my right.
Around me here at court
I find dislike and defamation,
And now an act of infamy
Has roused my indignation:
The casket, in which I hold,
Sire, the pearls I own,
Diff'rent objects, treasured keepsakes,
Of worth to myself alone . . .
'T has disappeared, my Lord,
I have been robbed, my Lord!
Oh help me to find it!
I demand it of your Majesty, the King!

(*The King gets up, slowly, takes a
casket from the table and offers it
to the Queen.*)

PHILIP

What you have lost, my Lady,
Here it is.

ELIZABETH

Ah!

PHILIP

I beg you to unlock it.
(*The Queen makes a sign of refusal.*)
I open it myself!
(*He breaks open the casket.*)

ELIZABETH (*aside*)
(Ah! May God be with me!)

PHILIP

'Tis the portrait of Carlo!
Would you care to explain it?
'Tis the portrait of Carlo!

ELIZABETH

Yes.

PHILIP

Amidst all your pearls?

ELIZABETH

Yes.

PHILIP

What! And you dare confirm your
guilt?

ELIZABETH

I dare it . . . yes!
Have you forgotten
That once to Carlo
In solemn promise
Was pledged my life?
Now by the holy will of the Almighty
I am your virtuous and loyal wife.
But now my foes suspect me,
And he, who should protect me,
Adds poison to their sting,
My noble husband, the King!

PHILIP

Your every gesture denotes defiance!
No doubt you now are certain
Of my humble compliance.
But my restraint may turn
To wildly flaming rage.
Then Heaven help both you and me!

ELIZABETH

But what has been my crime?

PHILIP

'Tis perjury!
If you reviled
And betrayed what is sacred;
If you defiled our holy union . . .
Then I swear it, I swear by God on
high,
To drown my shame in blood!

ELIZABETH

You raise my pity . . .

PHILIP

Ah! Spare your pity,
The pity of a harlot!

ELIZABETH (*fainting*)
Ah!

PHILIP
(*opening the door to the rear*)
Someone to help the Queen!

EBOLI
(*terrified at seeing the Queen lying
unconscious*)
(Ah! God forgive me! My Queen!)

RODRIGO (*to the King*)
Sire, you wield the power.
Over millions of humans:
Can it be true,
That in this vast domain the one
Whom you have failed to command
Is you?

FILIPPO (*Tra sè*)

(Ah! sii maledetto, sospetto fatale,
Opera d'un demòn, d'un demòn infernal.
(No! no! non macchiò la fè giurata . . .
La sua fierezza il dice a me!)

EBOLI (*Tra sè*)

(La perdei! . . . la perdei! . . .
Oh rimorso fatale!
Commettea un delitto infernal!
La perdei!)

RODRIGO (*Tra sè*)

(Omai d'oprar suonata è l'ora,
Folgor orrenda in ciel brillò,
Che per la Spagna un uomo muora
Lieto avvenir le lascerò.)

FILIPPO

No! no! non macchiò la fè giurata . . .
La sua fierezza il dice a me!)

ELISABETTA (*Rinvenendo*)

Che avvenne? O ciel! in pianto e duolo
Ognun, o madre, m'abbandonò.
Io son straniera in questo suol!
Più . . . sulla terra speme non ho!
Ognun ahimè! o madre mia, ognun
    quaggiù m'abbandonò,
Più speme omai ah! . . . che in ciel,
    in ciel non ho!

(*Il Re esce dopo breve esitazione. Rodrigo lo segue con gesto risoluto. Eboli resta sola con la Regina.*)

EBOLI

(*Gettandosi ai piedi d'Elisabetta*)

Pietà, perdon! per la rea che si pente.

ELISABETTA

Al mio piè! Voi! Qual colpa?

EBOLI

Ah! m'uccide il rimorso!
Torturato è il mio cor.
Angel del ciel, Regina augusta e pia,
Sappiate a qual demòn l'inferno vi dà
    in preda!
Quello scrigno . . . son io che l'involai.

ELISABETTA

Voi!

EBOLI

Sì, son io, son io che v'accusai!

ELISABETTA

Voi!

EBOLI

Sì . . . L'amor, il furor . . . L'odio che
    avea per voi . . .
La gelosia . . . crudel che straziavami
    il cor
Contro voi m'eccitâr!
Io Carlo amava! E Carlo m'ha sprezzata!

ELISABETTA

Voi l'amaste! Sorgete!

EBOLI

No! no! pietà di me! un'altra colpa!

ELISABETTA

Ancor!

EBOLI

Pietà! pietà! Il Re . . . non imprecate
    a me!
Sì sedotta! perduta! l'error che
    v'imputai . . .
Io . . . io stessa . . . avea . . . commesso!

ELISABETTA

Rendetemi la croce!
La corte vi convien lasciar col dì
    novello!
Fra l'esiglio ed il vel sceglier potrete!

(*Esce*)

(*Eboli si rialza.*)

EBOLI (*Con disperazione*)

Ah! più non vedrò . . .
Ah più mai non vedrò la Regina!
O don fatale, o don crudel
Che in suo furor mi fece il cielo!
Tu che ci fai sì vane, altere
Ti maledico, o mia beltà.
Versar, versar sol posso il pianto,
Speme non ho, soffrir dovrò!
Il mio delitto è orribil tanto
Che cancellar mai nol potrò!

PHILIP (*aside*)
(Infernal suspicion,
Eternal perdition;
Cursed be this evil spell
Of a demon in Hell!
No, no! She could not betray me.
Her noble bearing cannot lie.)

EBOLI (*aside*)
(It is I, it is I,
Who have doomed her forever!
What I did is too monstrous
A crime! Let me die!)

RODRIGO (*aside*)
(The time is here!
All doubt has ended.
A flash of lightning
Has rent the sky,
And without fear,
As Fate intended,
For God and Right
I have to die!)

PHILIP (*aside*)
(Now I know she never betrayed me,
Never degraded what is noble and
    true.)

ELIZABETH (*coming to*)
Where am I? Oh Heaven! . . .
In pain and sorrow,
Far from the land I knew long ago,
Alone, forsaken, in darkest night!
All now has ended
But torment and woe!
Alone, I suffer in pain and anguish.
Oh, take me back, oh land of mine!

(*After a moment of hesitation, the
    King leaves. With an obvious gesture
    of decision, Rodrigo follows him.
    Eboli remains alone with the Queen.*)

EBOLI
(*throwing herself at the Queen's feet*)
My Queen! In shame and horror
I ask for your mercy.

ELIZABETH
Why do you ask my mercy?

EBOLI
Ah, no longer can I bear it,
For my conscience is torn.
Angel of light, my Queen,
My royal Lady:
Your eyes are now beholding
A Fury sent by Satan.
Your casket . . .
'Twas I who stole it, I!

ELIZABETH
You?

EBOLI
Yes, for I had turned into a spy!

ELIZABETH
You!

EBOLI
Yes. What love could not possess,
My hatred would destroy!
Raving in jealous despair
I no longer could bear
The distress of my heart!
I loved Don Carlo,
And Carlo did reject me!

ELIZABETH
You have loved him? Arise!

EBOLI
No, no! My Queen, forgive me!
I have not told you . . .

ELIZABETH
What . . . more?!

EBOLI
Ah, mercy! Mercy! The King . . .
Your eyes impale my heart!
I, disgraced and forsaken . . .
The crime I blamed on you,
I, my Lady, have wrought myself!

ELIZABETH
The crucifix I gave you . . . !
(*Eboli hands it to her.*)
You will depart from court
Before the day is over!
Between exile and veil
You have the choice!
(*The Queen leaves. Eboli rises.*)

EBOLI (*in despair*)
Ah! The Queen has left me,
And now I have lost her forever!
Oh, dole of darkness,
Oh, boon of Hell,
That in his fury
Has fashioned a demon!
You wrought my beauty
To cast your spell!
Vainly I curse you,
Vainly I curse your gift from Hell!
My bitter tears, my desolation,
My tortured mind, my heart distraught
All my repentance, my desperation
Cannot undo what I have wrought!
Favor from Satan, vainly I curse you!
Beauty of mine, ah!

Ti maledico, ti maledico, o mia beltà,
Ah! ti maledico, o mia beltà.
O mia Regina, io t'immolai
Al folle error di questo cor.
Solo in un chiostro al mondo omai
Dovrò celar il mio dolor!
Ohimè! Ohimè! Oh mia Regina,
Solo in un chiostro al mondo omai
Dovrò celar il mio dolore! Ah!
Solo in un chiostro al mondo omai
Dovrò celar il mio dolor!
Oh ciel! E Carlo? a morte domani ...
Gran Dio! a morte andar vedrò!
Ah! un dì mi resta,
La speme m'arride,
Sia benedetto il ciel! Lo salverò!

### SCENA 2

*La Prigione di Don Carlo. Un oscuro sotterraneo, nel quale sono state gettate in fretta alcune suppellettili della Corte. In fondo cancello di ferro che separa la prigione da una corte che la domina e nella quale si veggono le guardie andare e venire. Una scalinata vi conduce dai piani superiori dell'edifizio.*

*(Don Carlo è assiso, col capo nelle mani, assorto nei suoi pensieri. Rodrigo entra, parla sottovoce ad alcuni uffiziali che si allontanano immediatamente. Egli contempla Don Carlo con tristezza. Questi ad un movimento di Rodrigo si scuote.)*

RODRIGO
Son io, mio Carlo.

DON CARLO
*(Dandogli la mano)*
O Rodrigo! io ti son ben grato
Di venir di Carlo alla prigion.

RODRIGO
Mio Carlo!

DON CARLO
Ben tu il sai! m'abbandonò il vigore!
D'Elisabetta l'amor ... mi tortura e m'uccide ...
No, più valor non ho pei viventi!
Oppressi, no, non fian più.

RODRIGO
Ah! noto appien ti sia l'affetto mio!
Uscir tu dêi da quest'orrendo avel.
Felice ancor io son se abbracciar ti poss'io!
Io ti salvai!

DON CARLO
Che di'?

RODRIGO *(Con emozione)*
Convien qui dirci addio.

*(Don Carlo resta immobile guardando Rodrigo con istupore.)*

O mio Carlo!
Per me giunto è il dì supremo,
No, mai più ci rivedrem;
Ci congiunga Iddio nel ciel,
Ei che premia i suoi fedel'.
Sul tuo ciglio il pianto io miro;
Lagrimar, così perchè?
No, fa cor, l'estremo spiro
Lieto è a chi morrà, morrà per te.

DON CARLO *(Tremando)*
Che parli tu di morte?

RODRIGO
Ascolta, il tempo stringe.
Rivolta ho già su me la folgore tremenda!
Tu più non sei oggi il rival del Re;
Il fiero agitator delle Fiandre ... son io!

DON CARLO
Chi potrà prestar fè?

RODRIGO
Le prove son tremende!
I fogli tuoi trovati in mio poter ...
Della ribellion testimoni son chiari,
E questo capo al certo a prezzo è messo già.

*(Due uomini discendono la scalinata della prigione. Uno d'essi è vestito dell' abito del Sant'Uffizio; l'altro è armato d'un archibugio. Si fermano un momento e si mostrano Don Carlo e Rodrigo che non li vedono.)*

Vainly I curse you, beauty from Hell!
Lonely and regal, oh see my crying,
You whom my madness sought to destroy
Pride, once so haughty, sinful and lying,
Now turned to shame, to gloom my joy!
Farewell, farewell, my Queen, forever!
Silent, the cloister
Witness my torment,
Hear my repentance,
Endless, undying, ah!
Only the cloister
Shall know my despair,
And God alone shall hear me cry!
Oh God! And Carlos? He . . . perish . . .
Tomorrow, and I myself
Shall be to blame?
Ah, I still can save him!
One ray of hope is shining:
Heaven, oh help me now!
He must be free! He shall not die!

### SCENE 2

*The prison of Don Carlo. A dark dungeon, hastily furnished with a few appropriate objects. Through the iron bars which separate the prison from the courtyard beyond we see guards pacing up and down. A small stairway leads from the courtyard up to the higher parts of the building.*

*(Don Carlo is sitting, deep in thought. Rodrigo enters, whispering to some officials who withdraw immediately. He sadly looks at Carlo who, aware of a visitor, moves slightly.)*

RODRIGO
'Tis I, O Carlo.

DON CARLO
*(extending his hand to him)*
O Rodrigo! I am most grateful
That you came to your unhappy friend.

RODRIGO
My Carlo!

DON CARLO
You must know that all my strength
Has left me. My heart by hopeless
  love has been strangled and broken.
No, my life is useless and empty.
But you continue to fight
For truth and human right.

RODRIGO
Carlo, you fill my heart
With grief and sorrow.
You have to leave
This place of gloom and death.
And yet, my heart is glad
For the chance to behold you.
I saved your life!

DON CARLO
My life?

RODRIGO *(deeply moved)*
'Tis for the last time,
For we shall part forever.
*(Don Carlo is stunned and looks at Rodrigo without making a move.)*
Oh, my Carlo!
Yes, my life will soon be ended,
And we never meet again
Till to God we have ascended,
Reunited in His reign.
On your brow I see your sorrow.
Bitter tears your eyes bedew.
Oh, take heart, yes, take heart!
Almighty Heaven will smile upon him,
Who gave his life to die for you.

DON CARLO_ *(worried)*
Why do you speak of dying?

RODRIGO
I'll tell you, but we must hurry.
The tide has turned, and I
Am now the leading culprit.
You now are free
Of all distrust and doubt:
He who has wrought rebellion
In Flanders . . . 'tis I!

DON CARLO
Who'd believe such a lie?

RODRIGO
The proof is overwhelming.
All your papers were found in my possession,
Clear and decisive proof
Of revolt and rebellion.
This morning, a price has been placed
Upon my head.
*(Two men are seen descending the stairway into the courtyard. One of them is an official of the Inquisition, the other holds a firearm. They stop a moment to discuss Don Carlo and Rodrigo who remain unaware of their presence.)*

DON CARLO

Svelar vo' tutto al Re.

RODRIGO

No, ti serba alla Fiandra,
Ti serba alla grand'opra, tu al dovrai
compire . . .
Un nuovo secol d'ôr rinascer tu farai;
Regnare tu dovevi, ed io morir per te.

(*L'uomo ch'è armato d'un archibugio mira Rodrigo e fa fuoco.*)

DON CARLO (*Atterrito*)

Ciel! la morte! per chi mai?

RODRIGO

(*Ferito mortalmente*)

Per me! La vendetta del Re tardare
non potea!

(*Cade nelle braccia di Don Carlo*)

DON CARLO

Gran Dio!

RODRIGO

O Carlo, ascolta, la madre t'aspetta a
San Giusto doman;
Tutto ella sa . . . Ah! la terra mi man-
ca . . .
Carlo mio, a me porgi la man!
Io morrò, ma lieto in core,
Chè potei così serbar
Alla Spagna un salvatore!
Ah! di me . . . non ti scordar!
Regnare tu dovevi, ed io morir per te.
Ah! la terra mi manca . . . la mano a
me . . .
Ah! salva la Fiandra . . . Carlo, addio,
ah! ah!

(*Rodrigo muore. Don Carlo cade dis-
peratamente sul corpo di Rodrigo.
Entra Filippo.*)

FILIPPO

Mio Carlo, a te la spada io rendo.

DON CARLO (*Con desolazione*)

Arretra! la tua man di sangue è intrisa
Una fraterna fede ci unia!
. . . Orror!

Ei m'amava! La vita sua per me sacrificò!

FILIPPO

(*Commosso, scoprendosi il capo davanti il corpo di Rodrigo*)

Presagio mio feral!

DON CARLO

Tu più figlio non hai!
I regni miei stan presso a lui!

FILIPPO

(*Contemplando Rodrigo*)

Chi rende a me quell'uom, chi rende
a me quell'uom?

(*S'ode suonare a stormo*)

GRANDI DI SPAGNA

Ciel! suona a stormo!

CORO DI POPOLO

Perir dovrà chi d'arrestarci attenti!
feriam!
Feriam! feriam, non abbia alcun pietà!
Tremar dovrà e curvar la testa davanti al popol ultor!

CONTE DI LERMA

Il popol è in furor!
È l'Infante ch'ei vuol!

FILIPPO

Si schiudan le porte!

CONTE DI LERMA E GRANDI DI SPAGNA

Ciel!

FILIPPO

Obbedite! Io lo vo'!
(*Il popolo entra furiosamente in
scena.*)

CORO DI POPOLO

Feriam! feriam!
Feriam, più niun . . . ci arresta! feriam!
Feriam, nè tema, nè pietà!
Tremar dovrà e curvar la testa davanti
al popol ultor!

EBOLI

(*Mascherata a Don Carlo*)

Va! fuggi!

FILIPPO

Che volete?

CORO

L'Infante!

**DON CARLO**

I must inform the King.

**RODRIGO**

No, remember our Flanders!
Remember them, my Carlo!
You are their sole defender.
In bright and radiant splendor
Our dream will yet come true!
Your life belongs to freedom,
While I must die for you.

(*The man carrying the firearm has taken aim at Rodrigo and fires.*)

**DON CARLO** (*terrified*)

God! A bullet . . . but for whom?

**RODRIGO** (*mortally wounded*)

For me . . . the revenge of the King . . .

(*sinking into Carlo's arms*)

. . . he did not lose a moment!

**DON CARLO**

Oh God!

**RODRIGO**

One word yet, my Carlo . . .
Your mother awaits you
At the cloister today.
She has been told . . .
Ah . . . my senses are waning . . .
Oh, my friend, once more
Give me your hand!
I shall die happy, contented,
For my life I give for Spain.
Carlo's death I have prevented,
And his stars shine once again!
My friend . . . remember me!
Your life belongs to freedom,
And I must die for you, ah!
I see you no longer . . .
Give me your hand, your hand . . .
Remember Flanders, O Carlo! . . .
Farewell, ah! farewell . . .

(*Rodrigo dies. Carlo throws himself across his lifeless body. King Philip enters with the Count of Lerma, Eboli, and other people of his entourage.*)

**PHILIP**

Don Carlo, I hand you back your sword.

**DON CARLO** (*in despair*)

Go from me!
Your hands are dripping with blood.
Assassin! Callous and cold,
You have murdered my brother,

Him who loved me,
Him who kept faith with me,
Even in death!

**PHILIP**

My son, I lose him, too!

**DON CARLO**

Do not call me your son!
No tie is left between you and me!

**PHILIP**

(*looking at Rodrigo*)

Where can I find anew
A man so great and true?

(*The storm-bells are heard.*)

**CHORUS OF GRANDEES**

Hear! Such commotion!

**CHORUS OF THE PEOPLE**

(*off-stage*)

Be free at last!
Let no one dare oppose us!
To arms! And mortal terror
Shall strike his heart,
Fear of the people's revenge.

**LERMA**

The crowd is in revolt.
They shout for the Prince.

**PHILIP**

Go, open the portals!

**LERMA AND THE GRANDEES**

Sire!

**PHILIP**

I command you. Do as I say!

(*A furious crowd is rushing onstage.*)

**CHORUS OF THE PEOPLE**

To arms! To arms!
No one will oppose us!
May terror strike their heart,
Fear of the people's revenge.

**EBOLI**

(*wearing a mask, to Don Carlo*)

Flee, Carlo!

**PHILIP**

What do you want?

**CHORUS OF THE PEOPLE**

The Crown-Prince!

FILIPPO

(*Additando Don Carlo*)

Egli qui sta!

INQUISITORE

Sacrilegio infame!

CORO DI POPOLO

(*Arretrando*)

Il Gran Inquisitor!

INQUISITORE

Vi prostrate innanzi al Re,
Che Dio protegge!
Vi prostrate! A terra!

FILIPPO

A terra!

INQUISITORE

Vi prostrate! A terra!

CORO DI POPOLO

(*Cadendo in ginocchio*)

Signor, di noi pietà!

FILIPPO

Gran Dio, sia gloria a Te! . . .

CONTE DI LERMA

Evviva il Re! Evviva il Re! . . .

FILIPPO

Gran Dio, sia gloria a Te! . . .

GRANDI DI SPAGNA

Evviva il Re!

CORO DI POPOLO

Signor, pietà!

(*Il Grande Inquisitore scende verso
Filippo che va incontro a lui in
mezzo al popolo genuflesso.*)

## ATTO QUINTO

*Il Chiostro del Convento di San Giusto
come nell'Atto Primo. Notte. Chiaro
di luna.*

(*Elisabetta entra lentamente, assorta
nei suoi pensieri, s'avvicina alla tomba di Carlo V e s'inginocchia.*)

ELISABETTA

Tu che le vanità conoscesti del mondo
E godi nell'avel il riposo profondo,
S'ancor si piange in cielo, piangi sul
mio dolore,
E porta il pianto mio al trono del
Signor.
Carlo qui verrà! Sì! Che parta e scordi
omai . . .
A Posa di vegliar sui giorni suoi giurai.
Ei segua il suo destin, la gloria il trac-
cerà.
Per me, la mia giornata a sera è giunta
già!
Francia, nobile suol, sì caro a'miei
verd'anni!
Fontainebleau! . . . vêr voi schiude il
pensier i vanni.
Eterno giuro d'amor là Dio da me
ascoltò,
E quest'eternità un giorno sol durò.
Tra voi, vaghi giardin di questa terra
ibéra,
Se Carlo ancor dovrà fermar i passi
a sera,
Che le zolle, i ruscelli, i fonti, i boschi,
i fior,
Con le lor armonie cantino il nostro
amor.
Addio, addio bei sogni d'ôr, illusion
perduta!
Il nodo si spezzô, la luce è fatta muta!
Addio, addio, verd'anni, ancor!
Cedendo al duol crudel!
Il cor ha un sol desir: la pace dell'-
avel!
Tu che le vanità conoscesti del mondo
E godi nell'avel il riposo profondo,
S'ancor si piange in cielo, piangi sul
mio dolore,
E porta il pianto mio a' pie' del Signor.

DON CARLO

È dessa!

ELISABETTA

Un detto, un sol; al ciel io raccomando
Il pellegrin che parte; e poi sol vi do-
mando

PHILIP
(*pointing to Don Carlo*)
Here is my son.

GRAND INQUISITOR
(*appearing suddenly*)
Infamy infernal!
(*The people recede before the Grand Inquisitor.*)

CHORUS OF THE PEOPLE
The Grand Inquisitor!

GRAND INQUISITOR
On your knees before the King!
The Lord protects him.
On your knees! Surrender!

PHILIP
Surrender!

GRAND INQUISITOR
On your knees! Surrender!
(*The people fall to their knees.*)

CHORUS OF THE PEOPLE
Oh Lord! Mercy, oh Sire!

PHILIP
Oh God, great is Thy name.

LERMA
Long live the King! Long live the King!

PHILIP
Oh God, great is Thy name.

CHORUS OF THE GRANDEES
(*with drawn swords*)
Long live the King!

CHORUS OF THE PEOPLE
Oh Lord! Have mercy!

(*The Grand Inquisitor descends towards Philip, who goes towards him among the kneeling crowd.*)

## ACT FIVE

*The Cloister of the Monastery of St. Just (same as Act I). It is night, brightened by moonlight.*

(*Elizabeth enters slowly, absorbed in her thoughts. She approaches the tomb of Charles V and kneels in front of it.*)

ELIZABETH
You, who spurned all the might
Which the world has to offer,
You found eternal peace in this tomb,
  cold and silent!
Blinded by tears, oh Father,
I raise my eyes to Heaven.
Grant me Thy aid
And ease my sorrow, gracious Lord!
Carlo will come soon.
Yes, in Flanders he will forget me.
To Posa I had sworn
To think of Carlo's future.
He must pursue his way,
And his stars are shining bright.
For me, the days are fading
And slowly turn to night.
France! Oh noble soil,
That saw my youthful yearning . . .
My Fontainebleau, where my thoughts
Are now returning.
Eternal love I swore
To one who went away:
Eternity, alas, did only last a day!
Gentle gardens of Spain,
Whose flowers I befriended,
If Carlo once again
Should dream of what has ended,
Every whisper, every sound
From your tender leaves shall recall
That there once was a Queen,
Whose love did never pall!
'Tis over, all now is gone,
All my hope has vanished.
The sky is filled with clouds,
And the wings of the night
Have descended upon me.
Oh memory of sunlight,
Torment me no more!
Descend, oh final doom!
My heart knows only one desire:
The darkness of the tomb!
You, who spurned all the might
That the world has to offer,
You found eternal peace
In this tomb, cold and silent:
Blinded by tears, oh Father,
I raise my eyes to Heaven!
Ah, see me grieving!
Grant me Thy aid, oh Lord!

DON CARLO (*entering*)
Elizabeth!

ELIZABETH
O Carlo, my son, at last
The hour has come,
And you will go to Flanders.

È l'obblio e la vita.

###### DON CARLO

Sì, forte esser vogl'io;
Ma quando è infranto amore
Pria della morte uccide.

###### ELISABETTA

No, pensate a Rodrigo.
Non è per folli idee,
Ch'ei si sacrificò!

###### DON CARLO

Sulla terra fiamminga,
Io vo' che a lui s'innalzi sublime, eccel-
so avel,
Qual mai ne ottenne un re tanto nobil
e bel.

###### ELISABETTA

I fior del paradiso a lui sorrideranno!

###### DON CARLO

Vago sogno m'arrise! ei sparve,
                        (*Cupo*)
E nell'affanno un rogo appar a me,
Che spinge vampe al ciel.
Di sangue tinto un rio, resi i campi un
avel,
Un popolo che muor, e a me la man
protende,
Siccome a Redentor, nei dì della sven-
tura.
A lui n'andrò beato, se, spento o vinci-
tor,
Plauso, o pianto m'avrò dal tuo me-
more cor!

###### ELISABETTA (*Con entusiasmo*)

Sì . . . l'eroismo è questo e la sua sacra
fiamma!
L'amor . . . degno di noi, l'amor che i
forti infiamma!
Ei . . . fa dell'uomo un Dio!
Va . . . di più non tardar! va . . . va
. . .va! . . . sali il Calvario
E salva un popolo che muor!

###### DON CARLO

Si . . . con la voce tua quella gente
m'appella
E . . . se morrò per lei, la mia morte
fia bella!

###### ELISABETTA

Il popol salva!
Va . . . va, di più non tardar!

###### DON CARLO

Ma pria di questo dì alcun poter uman
Disgiunta non avria la mia dalla tua
man!
Ma vinto in sì gran dì l'onor ha in me
l'amore;
Impresa a questa par rinnova e mente
e core!
Non vedi, Elisabetta! io ti stringo al
mio sen,
Nè mia virtù vacilla, nè ad essa
mancherò!
Or che tutto finì e la man io ritiro dalla
tua man . . .
Tu piangi?

###### ELISABETTA

Si, piango, ma t'ammiro,
Il pianto gli è dell'alma, e veder tu lo
puoi,
Qual san pianto versar . . . le donne
per gli eroi!

###### ELISABETTA E DON CARLO

Ma lassù ci vedremo in un mondo
migliore,
Dell'avvenir eterno suonan per noi già
l'ore;
E là noi troverem nel grembo del
Signor . . .
Il sospirato ben che fugge in terra
ognor!

Addio! per sempre addio, per sempre!
(*Entrano Filippo, Il Grande Inquisitore, e Familiari del Santo Uffizio.*)

###### FILIPPO

(*Prendendo il braccio della Regina*)

Sì, per sempre!
Io voglio un doppio sacrifizio!
Il dover mio farò.
                  (*All'Inquisitore*)

Ma voi?

###### IL GRANDE INQUISITORE

Il Santo Uffizio il suo farà.

###### ELISABETTA

Ciel!

###### IL GRANDE INQUISITORE

(*Ai familiari del Santo Uffizio, additando Don Carlo*)

Guardie! . . .

And soon your bitter sorrow
Will have faded in oblivion.

DON CARLO

Yes, my courage will return.
But once a heart is broken,
No courage can restore it.

ELIZABETH

No! Remember Rodrigo!
'Tis not for foolish dreams
That he sacrificed his life.

DON CARLO

On the fields of Flanders
I vow to fashion him
A monument so great, so mighty,
As has never ennobled a king.

ELIZABETH

Like flowers on fragrant breezes
Our tender thoughts will find him.

DON CARLO

In my dreams I can see him . . .
Oh terror! (darkly)
Now, like a nightmare,
I see a monstrous pyre
Ablaze with roaring fire . . .
A river dark with blood,
Its current rising higher, . . .
A people in despair,
Their bony hands extended,
Begging in anguished prayer
Their torture may be ended.
I'll lead my people onward,
With honor to win or die,
And to find what in hate
Here my fate would deny!

ELIZABETH (exaltedly)

Bring to your people their freedom,
Let Freedom's glory guide you!
My love shall ride beside you
And brace your dauntless heart.
High on the stars keep your eye!
Go now and tarry no more, ah!,
As onward you ride as the savior
Of a land which without you will die!

DON CARLO

Sing, and your voice shall inspire
My devotion to duty!
Dying for you is to drown
In an ocean of beauty!

ELIZABETH

Redeem your people!
Go, and tarry no more!

DON CARLO

My love, before today,
No power on earth could part
From you, who held in sway
My tortured, broken heart:
Now I have found the key
To what my fate intended.
At last now my mind is free,
And my despair is ended.
Elizabeth, I can behold you
And embrace you at last,
Blameless, and proud to face you,
Now that my die is cast!
Yes, at last we are free.
But your eyes speak of grief
And silent pain . . . you are weeping?

ELIZABETH

Yes, tears of pride and parting,
The tears of tender sorrow,
Tears you always will find,
Where soldiers bid farewell
To those who must stay behind.

ELIZABETH AND DON CARLO

But beyond, up in Heaven,
While its wonders surround us,
There, where in love eternal
His mighty will has bound us,
At last He will unite
And take unto His heart
Those whom the stars had joined,
But man has forced apart.
On that day filled with joy,
Day that knows no tomorrow,
We remember no more
Past despair, former sorrow.
Farewell forever! Farewell forever!

(Enter the King with the Grand Inquisitor and several officials of the Inquisition.)

PHILIP

(taking the Queen by the arm)

Yes, forever!
A two-fold sacrifice I offer!
I shall do my duty.
(to the Grand Inquisitor) And you?

GRAND INQUISITOR

The holy Council will perform its task.

ELIZABETH

Heaven!

GRAND INQUISITOR

(to the officials of the Inquisition, pointing to Don Carlo)
Guards!

#### DON CARLO

Dio mi vendicherà!
Il tribunal di sangue
Sua mano spezzerà!

(*Don Carlo, difendendosi, indietreggia
verso la tomba di Carlo Quinto. Il
cancello s'apre. Un Frate appare; è
Carlo Quinto col manto e colla corona reale.*)

#### IL FRATE

Il duolo della terra
Nel chiostro ancor ci segue,
Solo del cor la guerra
In ciel si calmerà!

#### INQUISITORE

È la voce di Carlo!

#### QUATTRO FAMILIARI DEL
#### SANTO UFFIZIO

È Carlo Quinto!

#### FILIPPO (*Spaventato*)

Mio padre!

#### ELISABETTA

Oh ciel!

(*Carlo Quinto trascina nel chiostro
Don Carlo smarrito.*)

## FINE DELL' OPERA

**DON CARLO**

Heaven will avenge my death.
I shall defy your terror
Until my final breath.

(*Don Carlo, fending off the officials,
retreats to the tomb of Charles V.
T e gate of the tomb opens, and the
Friar, now clearly recognizable as
the former emperor Charles V,
wearing his regalia and crown, appears.*)

**THE FRIAR**

The anguish of the mortal
Will even haunt the temple.
Only the holy portal
Can grant us final peace.

**GRAND INQUISITOR**

'Tis the voice of King Charles!

**OFFICIALS OF THE INQUISITION**

'Tis Charles the Fifth!

**PHILIP** (*terrified*)

My father!

**ELIZABETH**

Oh God!

(*Charles V pulls Don Carlo into the
cloister.*)

# END OF THE OPERA